CW01668957

# Spelling Patterns

B. V. Allan

Illustrated by A. & W. Rodger

CollinsEducational
*An imprint of* HarperCollins*Publishers*

## Exercise 1

**1** Listen to your teacher reading the words.
**2** Read the words with your teacher.
**3** Read the words to yourself and choose a key word to illustrate in your spelling book.
**4** Now do the work in your spelling book. Put the words on one page and the picture on the opposite page.

Do the four parts of **Exercise 1** whenever you see this signal. 

**Acknowledgements**

I am indebted to the London Word Blind Centre for Dyslexic Children, run by the Invalid Children's Aid Association, for my initial knowledge of and interest in spelling patterns. I am equally indebted to all the children I have taught, in London, Edinburgh, East Lothian and Lancashire.

**A language for life** (Report of the Committee of Inquiry appointed by the Secretary of State for Education and Science, under the chairmanship of Sir Alan Bullock FBA, 1975)

11.12 'We believe that . . . children should acquire . . . a knowledge of spelling rules and an ability to generalise about words.'

11.48 (Attention should be paid to) . . . 'details of word structure, similarities of letter sequence, and the varying probabilities of such sequences.'

**References**

*Dr. Seuss Beginner Books* (Collins)
B. V. Allan, *Logical Spelling* (Collins)
D. H. Stott, *Programmed Reading Kit* (Holmes McDougall)
B. V. Allan, *Spelling Patterns Practice Sheets* (Collins)

Published by CollinsEducational
77–85 Fulham Palace Road, London W6 8JB

© 1979 B. V. Allan
0 00 314250 7
Printed in Hong Kong

Tenth impression 1993
CollinsEducational
London and Glasgow

All rights reserved
No part of this publication may be reproduced, stored in a retrieval system, or transmitted, in any form or by any means, electronic, mechanical, photocopying, recording or otherwise, without the prior permission of the copyright owner.

# Contents

# Part I — patterns with vowels

## ing

| | | | |
|---|---|---|---|
| box | boxing | win | winning |
| tell | telling | hit | hitting |
| ask | asking | sit | sitting |
| sing | singing | bat | batting |
| bring | bringing | pat | patting |
| cash | cashing | bet | betting |
| dash | dashing | get | getting |
| spell | spelling | let | letting |
| shop | shopping | | |

boxing

### Exercise 1

### Exercise 2

Write down all the **ing** words you can see illustrated in this picture.

### Exercise 3

Write these sentences, filling in the missing words.

**1** He was _ _ _ _ _ _ _ _ a song.
**2** Tom was _ _ _ _ _ _ _ _ his dog.
**3** Mum had a _ _ _ _ _ _ _ _ _ bag at the shops.
**4** Jill was _ _ _ _ _ _ _ _ on the bench.
**5** Bill and Tom were _ _ _ _ _ _ _ _ at cricket.

| | |
|---|---|
| pin | pinned |
| tin | tinned |
| pass | passed |
| lash | lashed |
| ask | asked |
| miss | missed |
| kiss | kissed |
| wish | wished |
| push | pushed |
| kill | killed |
| fill | filled |

| | |
|---|---|
| slip | slipped |
| tip | tipped |
| trip | tripped |
| tap | tapped |
| hop | hopped |
| pop | popped |

legged
ragged
rugged
padded
plodded
nodded
nested
tested

**ed**

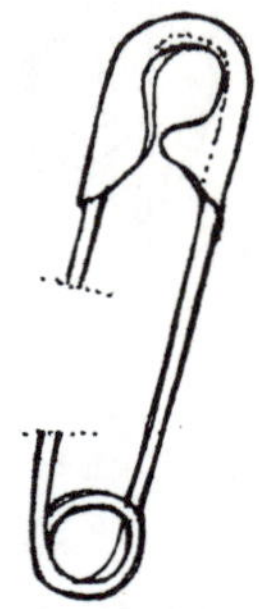

pinned

## Exercise 1

## Exercise 2

Write down all the **ed** words you can see illustrated in this picture.

## Exercise 3

Write these sentences, filling in the missing words.

1 Tim ________ his glass with milk.
2 Soft things are often ________ .
3 Dan ________ on his left leg.
4 Ann ________ the test.
5 Mum ________ up the step.

# er

dinner

| | | | |
|---|---|---|---|
| kill | killer | dinner | supper |
| mad | madder | winter | ever |
| sad | sadder | summer | never |
| win | winner | father | clever |
| hop | hopper | mother | river |
| pop | popper | brother | silver |
| big | bigger | sister | number |
| run | runner | other | person |
| | | another | finger |
| | | under | after |

## Exercise 1

## Exercise 2

Write down all the **er** words you can see illustrated in this picture.

## Exercise 3

Write these sentences, filling in the missing words.

**1** He had ham and chips for _ _ _ _ _ _ .
**2** In _ _ _ _ _ _ _ it is hot.
**3** A hand has 5 _ _ _ _ _ _ _ s.
**4** 6 is a _ _ _ _ _ _ _ .
**5** A _ _ _ _ _ _ _ kills.

| | | |
|---|---|---|
| fat | fatter | fattest |
| fast | faster | fastest |
| mad | madder | maddest |
| sad | sadder | saddest |
| big | bigger | biggest |
| odd | odder | oddest |
| fit | fitter | fittest |
| hot | hotter | hottest |
| dull | duller | dullest |
| full | fuller | fullest |

fattest

## Exercise 1

## Exercise 2

Write down all the **est** words you can see illustrated in this picture.

## Exercise 3

Write these sentences, filling in the missing words.

1 The ______________ runner got the cup.
2 The ______________ man was bigger than the rest.
3 The ____________ boy was odder than the others.
4 Tim was hot, Bill was hotter but dad was ______________ .
5 The ______________ glass was filled to the top.

# y

| | | | |
|---|---|---|---|
| mum | mummy | lorry | jelly |
| dad | daddy | sorry | jolly |
| fat | fatty | marry | holly |
| sun | sunny | hurry | puppy |
| fun | funny | happy | windy |
| nut | nutty | silly | nasty |
| skin | skinny | penny | rusty |
| hill | hilly | | |

lorry

## Exercise 1

## Exercise 2

Write down all the **y** words you can see illustrated in this picture.

## Exercise 3

Write these sentences, filling in the missing words.

**1** The _ _ _ _ _ could not get up the hill.
**2** Mummy and _ _ _ _ _ should help us to spell.
**3** You would be _ _ _ _ _ if you let _ _ _ _ _ prick you.
**4** A comic is a _ _ _ _ _ man.

| | | | | | |
|---|---|---|---|---|---|
| feet | sweet | | sweeter | sweetest | |
| sheet | deep | | deeper | deepest | |
| street | feel | feeling | feeler | | |
| screen | seek | seeking | seeker | | |
| peel | feed | feeding | feeder | | |
| cheese | keep | keeping | keeper | | |
| freeze | need | needing | needed | | needy |
| bee | greed | | | | greedy |
| week | cheek | | | | cheeky |
| sheep | see | seeing | seen | | |
| green | seem | seeming | seemed | | |
| | meet | meeting | | | |

**ee**

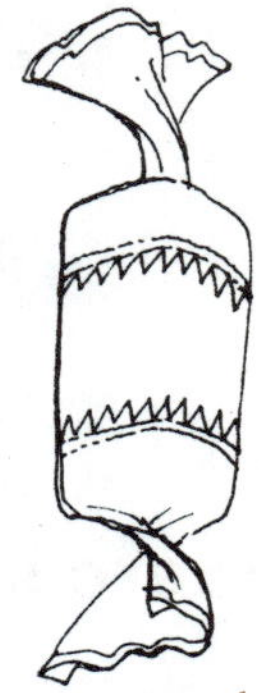

sweet

## Exercise 1

## Exercise 2

Write down all the **ee** words you can see illustrated in this picture.

## Exercise 3

Write these sentences, filling in the missing words.

**1** A _ _ _ _ _ is an animal.
**2** A _ _ _ is an insect.
**3** The _ _ _ _ _ _ has many shops.
**4** Tom did not have any Cheddar _ _ _ _ _ _ .
**5** I _ _ _ _ hot in the sun.

# ou

house

| | | | | |
|---|---|---|---|---|
| house | our | shout | amount | mound |
| mouse | hour | stout | mountain | wound |
| mouth | sour | about | fountain | bound |
| south | flour | trout | found | ground |
| loud | out | sprout | round | trousers |
| cloud | scout | count | pound | |
| proud | spout | mount | sound | |

## Exercise 1

## Exercise 2

Write down all the **ou** words you can see illustrated in this picture.

## Exercise 3

Write these sentences, filling in the missing words.

**1** A __ __ __ __ __ is a fish.
**2** A __ __ __ __ __ is an animal.
**3** A thing that is not sweet is __ __ __ __ .
**4** A __ __ __ __ __ __ __ __ is a very big hill.
**5** A ring is __ __ __ __ __ .

## ea

| | | | | |
|---|---|---|---|---|
| pea | beat | clean | teach | hear |
| sea | seat | each | teacher | dear |
| tea | meat | beach | team | fear |
| east | heat | reach | steam | near |
| beast | wheat | leave | stream | rear |
| least | neat | leaf | scream | reason |
| feast | meal | leap | dream | season |
| please | seal | heap | lead | peace |
| ease | real | cheap | read | peaceful |
| easy | steal | weak | bead | peacefully |
| eat | mean | speak | ear | |

pea

### Exercise 1

### Exercise 2

Write down all the **ea** words you can see illustrated in this picture.

### Exercise 3

Write these sentences, filling in the missing words.

1 A ________ is an animal.
2 We sit on a ________ .
3 I can ________ a loud bang with my ______ .
4 Summer is our hot ____________ .

# ar

| | | | | | |
|---|---|---|---|---|---|
| scarf | art | farm | farmer | farming | farmed |
| scar | tart | march | marcher | marching | marched |
| star | start | mark | marker | marking | marked |
| car | barn | bark | barker | barking | barked |
| far | yarn | park | | parking | parked |
| bar | ark | spark | | sparking | sparked |
| tar | dark | start | starter | starting | started |
| arm | park | | | | |
| farm | | smart | smarter | smartest | |
| yard | | sharp | sharper | sharpest | are |

scarf

## Exercise 1

## Exercise 2

Write down all the **ar** words you can see illustrated in this picture.

## Exercise 3

Write these sentences, filling in the missing words.

**1** A ___ ___ ___ has four wheels.
**2** A ___ ___ ___ ___ has many animals and crops.
**3** The animals went into the ___ ___ ___ two by two.
**4** Ten, nine, eight, seven, six, five, four, three, two, one, blast off, the rocket will ___ ___ ___ ___ ___ .
**5** Ten and one ___ ___ ___ eleven.

# ay

| | | | |
|---|---|---|---|
| play | pay | spray | today |
| way | paying | crayon | yesterday |
| always | lay | stay | Sunday |
| away | laying | staying | Monday |
| may | gay | player | Tuesday |
| ray | hay | playful | Wednesday |
| tray | clay | playtime | Thursday |
| say | ray | day | Friday |
| saying | pray | daytime | Saturday |

play

## Exercise 1

## Exercise 2

Write down all the **ay** words you can see illustrated in this picture.

## Exercise 3

Write these sentences, filling in the missing words.

**1** A week has seven ___ ___ ___ s.
**2** Men ___ ___ ___ ___ cricket in summer.
**3** After ___ ___ ___ ___ ___ ___ it is Saturday.
**4** We ___ ___ ___ ___ to God.
**5** We can model things with ___ ___ ___ ___ .

# ai

chain

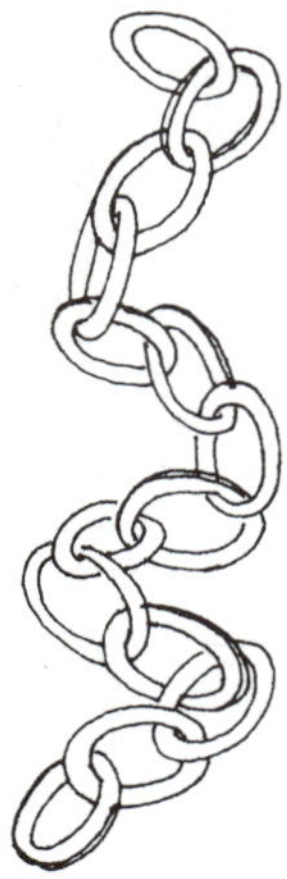

| | | | |
|---|---|---|---|
| chain | painless | nail | sailor |
| train | raining | mail | sailed |
| rain | rained | rail | laid |
| brain | rainy | railing | maid |
| Spain | plain | railway | paid |
| gain | plainly | pail | raid |
| again | explain | trail | afraid |
| regain | wait | trailer | paint |
| main | waiter | trailed | painter |
| remain | waited | sail | painted |
| pain | waiting | sailing | painting |
| painful | tail | | |

## Exercise 1

## Exercise 2

Write down all the **ai** words you can see illustrated in this picture.

## Exercise 3

Write these sentences, filling in the missing words.

**1** A _ _ _ _ _ runs on a railway track.
**2** If it _ _ _ _ s we may get wet.
**3** We have a _ _ _ _ at the end of each finger.
**4** The painter _ _ _ _ _ _ _ _ the house.
**5** A ship may _ _ _ _ on the sea.

| | | | |
|---|---|---|---|
| boat | goal | oak | toasting |
| coat | road | cloak | toasted |
| goat | toad | soak | roast |
| throat | load | soaking | roasting |
| float | loader | soaked | roasted |
| floating | loading | loaf | |
| floated | loaded | soap | |
| oats | coach | soapy | |
| coal | coaching | toast | |
| foal | coached | toaster | broad |

# oa

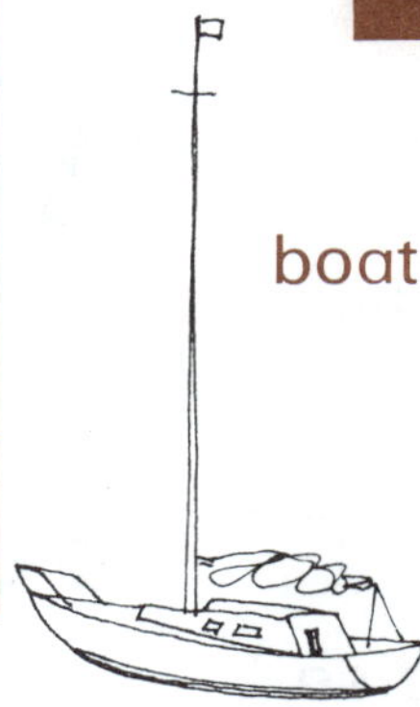
boat

## Exercise 1

## Exercise 2

Write down all the **oa** words you can see illustrated in this picture.

## Exercise 3

Write these sentences, filling in the missing words.

1 An __ __ __ is a tree.
2 A __ __ __ __ and a __ __ __ __ are animals.
3 A car travels along a __ __ __ __ .
4 A foal eats __ __ __ __ .
5 The footballer kicked the ball into the __ __ __ __ .

# y

fly

| | | | |
|---|---|---|---|
| by | fly | flying | nylon |
| my | try | trying | plywood |
| sky | fry | frying | supply |
| sty | cry | crying | satisfy |
| sly | dry | drying | multiply |
| shy | spy | spying | |
| | | dying | |

## Exercise 1

## Exercise 2

Write down all the **y** words you can see illustrated in this picture.

## Exercise 3

Write these sentences, filling in the missing words.

**1** A ___ ___ ___ is an insect.
**2** The sun is in the ___ ___ ___ .
**3** We ___ ___ ___ chips.
**4** A fox is ___ ___ ___ .
**5** Another way of saying 6 × 6 is ___ ___ ___ ___ ___ ___ ___ ___ 6 by 6.

| | | |
|---|---|---|
| cake | wave | made |
| make | save | safe |
| face | page | came |
| race | cage | name |
| take | gate | game |
| gave | late | |

# a—e

cake

## Exercise 1

## Exercise 2

Write down all the **a—e** words you can see illustrated in this picture.

## Exercise 3

Write these sentences, filling in the missing words.

**1** Mother bakes a _ _ _ _ .
**2** Football is a _ _ _ _ .
**3** Tom is a boy's _ _ _ _ .
**4** The fastest runner in the _ _ _ _ got the cup.
**5** We keep things _ _ _ _ in a _ _ _ _ .

# i—e

bike

| | | |
|---|---|---|
| bike | tide | white |
| fire | wide | wife |
| wire | ice | knife |
| like | nice | life |
| mine | mice | mile |
| nine | quite | smile |
| five | | |

## Exercise 1

## Exercise 2

Write down all the **i—e** words you can see illustrated in this picture.

## Exercise 3

Write these sentences, filling in the missing words.

**1** A _ _ _ _ has two wheels.
**2** Ten is the number after _ _ _ _ .
**3** _ _ _ _ is the number after four.
**4** We cut with a _ _ _ _ _ .
**5** _ _ _ _ are animals.

| | | |
|---|---|---|
| mole | smoke | home |
| hole | spoke | gnome |
| pole | bone | hope |
| nose | lone | rope |
| rose | alone | doze |
| joke | stone | rode |
| woke | | |

## o—e

mole

## Exercise 1

## Exercise 2

Write down all the **o—e** words you can see illustrated in this picture.

## Exercise 3

Write these sentences, filling in the missing words.

1 _ _ _ _ _ means no one is with you.
2 The man _ _ _ _ _ s his pipe.
3 A _ _ _ _ _ is a rock.
4 A _ _ _ _ is an animal.
5 The wheel of my bike has _ _ _ _ _ s.

# u—e

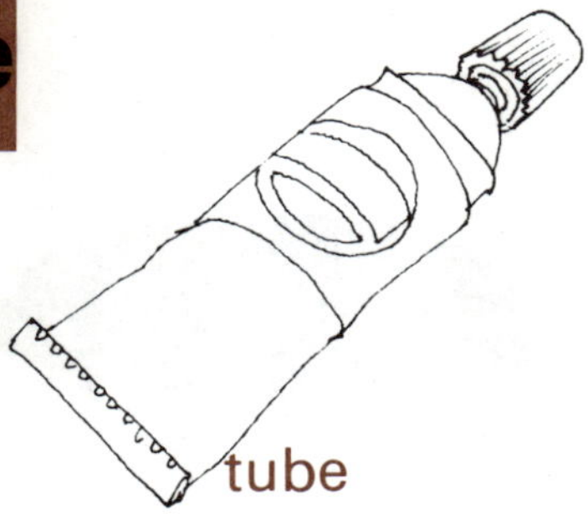

tube

| | | |
|---|---|---|
| tube | mule | fuse |
| cube | rule | refuse |
| tune | use | pure |
| June | amuse | cure |
| duke | excuse | rude |

## Exercise 1

## Exercise 2

Write down all the **u—e** words you can see illustrated in this picture.

## Exercise 3

Write these sentences, filling in the missing words.

**1** A __ __ __ __ has six sides.
**2** A __ __ __ __ is an animal.
**3** A funny person __ __ __ __ __ s us.
**4** We sing a __ __ __ __ .
**5** We __ __ __ a knife to cut with.

| | | | | |
|---|---|---|---|---|
| ball | call | calling | called | caller |
| all | fall | falling | | |
| hall | | | | |
| wall | tall | taller | tallest | |
| stall | small | smaller | smallest | |

## all

ball

## Exercise 1

## Exercise 2

Write down all the **all** words you can see illustrated in this picture.

## Exercise 3

Write these sentences, filling in the missing words.

1 Cricket is played with a bat and _ _ _ _ .
2 Humpty Dumpty had a bad _ _ _ _ .
3 An ant is _ _ _ _ _ _ _ than a bee.
4 The market _ _ _ _ _ sells plants with tall stalks.
5 "You must not walk and talk at _ _ _," said the teacher, putting away his chalk.

# igh

| | | | |
|---|---|---|---|
| light | knight | high | frighten |
| lighter | fight | higher | frightening |
| lightest | fighter | highest | frightened |
| lightly | fighting | might | frightful |
| slight | sigh | mighty | bright |
| slightly | sighing | thigh | brighter |
| flight | sighed | right | brightest |
| night | sight | fright | |

light

## Exercise 1

## Exercise 2

Write down all the **igh** words you can see illustrated in this picture.

## Exercise 3

Write these sentences, filling in the missing words.

**1** It is dark at _ _ _ _ _ but in daytime it is _ _ _ _ _ _.
**2** The four o'clock plane was the last _ _ _ _ _ _ to Paris.
**3** The huge beast _ _ _ _ _ _ _ _ _ _ everybody.
**4** He used his _ _ _ _ _ _ _ to light his pipe.

| | | | |
|---|---|---|---|
| cow | prowl | drown | tower |
| how | prowler | drowning | flower |
| now | prowling | drowned | shower |
| sow | prowled | clown | powder |
| bow | down | frown | towel |
| brow | town | frowning | vowel |
| owl | brown | frowned | trowel |
| howl | crown | crowd | allow |
| fowl | crowning | crowded | |
| | crowned | | |

# ow

cow

## Exercise 1

## Exercise 2

Write down all the **ow** words you can see illustrated in this picture.

## Exercise 3

Write these sentences, filling in the missing words.

1 A ___ ___ ___ is an animal.
2 An ___ ___ ___ is a bird.
3 Mother and father would not ___ ___ ___ ___ ___ my brother and sister to stay up late.
4 The other day I asked my mother for another ___ ___ ___ ___ ___ to dry myself.
5 We use a ___ ___ ___ ___ ___ ___ for gardening.

# le

| | | | |
|---|---|---|---|
| apple | sparkle | simple | single |
| bubble | angle | dazzle | able |
| candle | bangle | bottle | table |
| riddle | spangle | bundle | stable |
| middle | pickle | saddle | |
| fiddle | little | | |

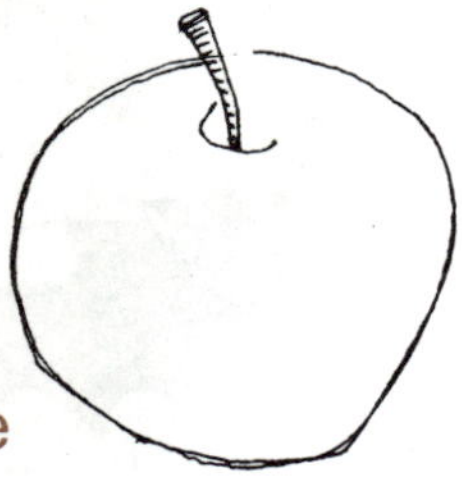

apple

## Exercise 1

## Exercise 2

Write down all the **le** words you can see illustrated in this picture.

## Exercise 3

Write these sentences, filling in the missing words.

**1** The children want a __ __ __ __ __ __ of pop.
**2** "Come and sit at the __ __ __ __ __," said mother.
**3** A __ __ __ __ __ __ gives light.
**4** We can play a tune on a __ __ __ __ __ __ .
**5** We can eat an __ __ __ __ __ .

## oo

| | | | | |
|---|---|---|---|---|
| too | boot | book | good | hoop |
| zoo | foot | took | stood | loop |
| food | soot | hook | wood | looped |
| noon | root | cook | wooden | room |
| moon | loot | cooked | wooded | broom |
| soon | cool | cooking | hood | balloon |
| tool | cooler | crooked | hooded | |
| pool | coolest | look | | |
| school | fool | looking | door | moor |
| loose | foolish | looked | floor | poor |

boot

## Exercise 1

## Exercise 2

Write down all the **oo** words you can see illustrated in this picture.

## Exercise 3

Write these sentences, filling in the missing words.

**1** The silly _ _ _ _ pulled a funny face.
**2** A _ _ _ _ runner can run at a fast pace.
**3** We read _ _ _ _ s to our teacher at _ _ _ _ _ _.
**4** She _ _ _ _ _ _ at her face in the mirror.

# or

horse

| | | | |
|---|---|---|---|
| horse | torn | sort | form |
| for | horn | fort | storm |
| fork | worn | short | torch |
| pork | story | sport | porch |
| cork | north | lord | doctor |
| stork | more | cord | afford |
| corn | | | |

## Exercise 1

## Exercise 2

Write down all the **or** words you can see illustrated in this picture.

## Exercise 3

Write these sentences, filling in the missing words.

1 The thunder and lightning made the __ __ __ __ __ very frightening.
2 The teacher gave us a __ __ __ __ __ about a circus and a clown in a gown with blue, violet and orange spots.
3 Running is a __ __ __ __ __ .
4 Pig meat is called __ __ __ __ .
5 When we are ill we call in the __ __ __ __ __ __ .

| | | | | |
|---|---|---|---|---|
| snow | show | crow | blowing | follow |
| snowing | showing | crowing | blown | following |
| snowed | showed | crowed | throw | followed |
| bowl | shown | grow | throwing | follower |
| bow | row | growing | thrown | yellow |
| low | rowing | grower | own | pillow |
| lower | rowed | grown | owner | arrow |
| lowest | flow | know | owning | barrow |
| slow | flowing | knowing | owned | narrow |
| slower | flowed | known | fellow | shadow |
| slowest | flown | blow | fellowship | elbow |

## ow

snow

## Exercise 1

## Exercise 2

Write down all the **ow** words you can see illustrated in this picture.

## Exercise 3

Write these sentences, filling in the missing words.

**1** Do you _ _ _ _ why the wind _ _ _ _ s?
**2** He can shoot with a _ _ _ and _ _ _ _ _ .
**3** _ _ _ _ _ _ is a colour.

# ture

| | | |
|---|---|---|
| creature | mixture | pasture |
| capture | fixture | future |
| picture | fracture | manufacture |
| adventure | structure | signature |
| scripture | texture | torture |
| puncture | furniture | vulture |

## Exercise 1

## Exercise 2

Write down all the **ture** words you can see illustrated in this picture.

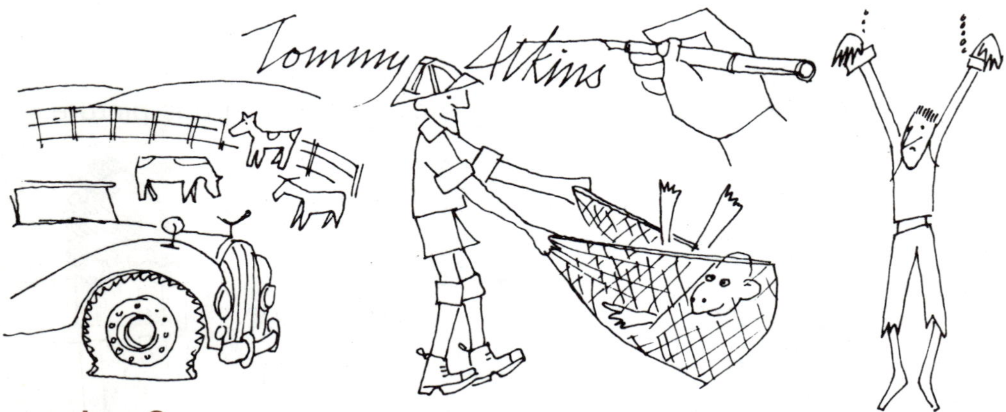


## Exercise 3

Write these sentences, filling in the missing words.

1 He could not use his shoe as his foot had a _ _ _ _ _ _ _ _ which needed a plaster cast.
2 Women often polish the _ _ _ _ _ _ _ _ _ in the house.
3 When his bike had a _ _ _ _ _ _ _ _ he had to mend the inner tube.
4 A _ _ _ _ _ _ _ is a bird of prey.
5 Cows graze in a _ _ _ _ _ _ _ .

| | | | |
|---|---|---|---|
| bread | instead | feather | stealth |
| head | thread | deaf | stealthy |
| dead | death | meant | measure |
| read | breath | heavy | treasure |
| ready | breathless | wealth | breakfast |
| already | leather | wealthy | pheasant |
| steady | weather | health | weapon |
| unsteady | heather | healthy | |

## ea

bread

### Exercise 1

### Exercise 2

Write down all the **ea** words you can see illustrated in this picture.

### Exercise 3

Write these sentences, filling in the missing words.

**1** Someone may cook the _ _ _ _ _ _ _ _ _ each morning.
**2** _ _ _ _ _ _ _ is something used for mending things.
**3** The teacher _ _ _ _ us a story.
**4** The _ _ _ _ _ _ _ is often hot in summer.
**5** A fat man will be _ _ _ _ _ .

# ir

bird

| | | |
|---|---|---|
| bird | shirt | sir |
| third | skirt | firm |
| thirteen | dirt | firmly |
| thirty | dirty | girl |
| thirst | stir | birth |
| thirsty | stirring | birthday |
| first | stirred | admiral |

## Exercise 1

## Exercise 2

Write down all the **ir** words you can see illustrated in this picture.

## Exercise 3

Write these sentences, filling in the missing words.

**1** She gave a glass of water to the _ _ _ _ _ _ _ man.
**2** The bear _ _ _ _ _ _ _ his honey with a big spoon.
**3** I gave my friend a present for his sixteenth _ _ _ _ _ _ _ _ .
**4** Number _ _ _ _ _ _ _ _ comes after twelve.
**5** The _ _ _ _ played in the mud and made her dress _ _ _ _ _ .

| | | |
|---|---|---|
| wasp | wallet | swan |
| was | wander | swamp |
| want | waddle | swallow |
| watch | waffle | |
| wash | wallow | |
| washing | | what |
| wand | | water |

# wa

wasp

## Exercise 1

## Exercise 2

Write down all the **wa** words you can see illustrated in this picture.

## Exercise 3

Write these sentences, filling in the missing words.

1 A _ _ _ _ is an insect seen in town and country.
2 A _ _ _ _ _ _ _ machine cleans our clothes.
3 A _ _ _ _ is a white bird.
4 When we _ _ _ _ _ a funny show, we laugh.
5 We chew food before we _ _ _ _ _ _ _ it.

# qua

quarrel

quarrel
qualify
quantity
quality
quarantine
squash
squat
squadron

## Exercise 1

## Exercise 2

Write down all the **qua** words you can see illustrated in this picture.

## Exercise 3

Write these sentences, filling in the missing words.

**1** We are put in ___ ___ ___ ___ ___ ___ ___ ___ ___ ___ when we are infectious.
**2** The thirsty child had a drink of ___ ___ ___ ___ ___ ___ .
**3** A group of airmen is called a ___ ___ ___ ___ ___ ___ ___ ___ .
**4** To argue is to ___ ___ ___ ___ ___ ___ ___ .
**5** To ___ ___ ___ ___ ___ is to bend down.

# air

| | | |
|---|---|---|
| chair | air | fairy |
| hair | airy | unfair |
| dairy | airless | pair |
| stair | airing | repair |
| stairway | aired | despair |
| staircase | fair | Claire |

chair

## Exercise 1

## Exercise 2

Write down all the **air** words you can see illustrated in this picture.

## Exercise 3

Write these sentences, filling in the missing words.

1 Two things are a __ __ __ __ .
2 Milk is bottled in a __ __ __ __ __ .
3 __ __ __ __ grows on the head.
4 To __ __ __ __ __ __ is to mend.
5 We sit on a __ __ __ __ __ .

# wor

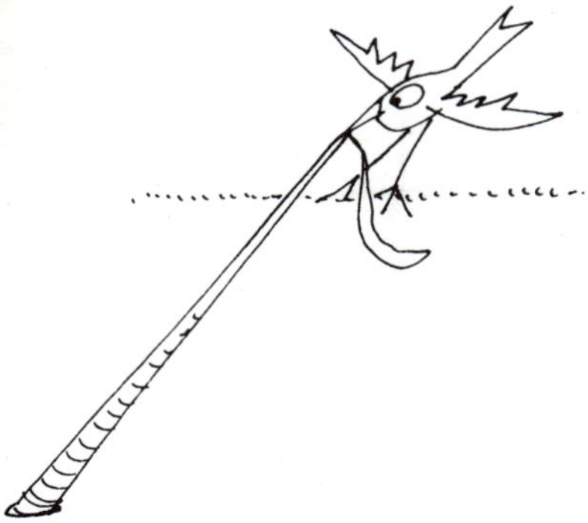

worm

| | |
|---|---|
| worm | worse |
| word | worst |
| world | work |
| worth | worker |
| worship | working |
| | worked |

## Exercise 1

## Exercise 2

Draw and label these pictures.

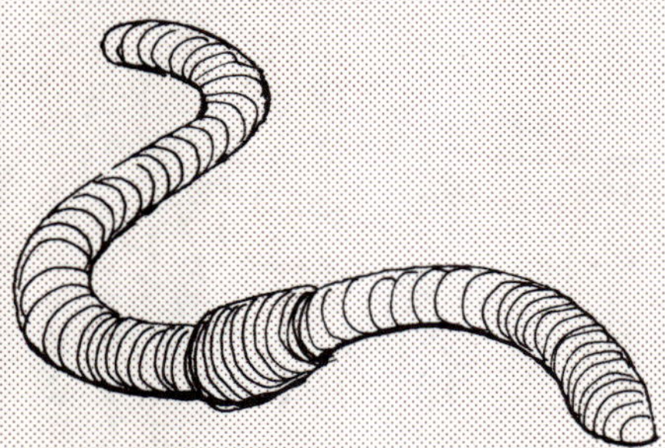

Choose two more words to draw and label.

## Exercise 3

Write these sentences, filling in the missing words.

**1** A man at work is called a _ _ _ _ _ _ .
**2** We _ _ _ _ _ _ _ God.
**3** The _ _ _ _ 'cat' is spelled c-a-t.
**4** A _ _ _ _ lives in the ground.
**5** Australia and Britain are at opposite sides of the _ _ _ _ _ .

fought
ought
nought
bought
brought
sought
thought

# ought

fought

## Exercise 1

## Exercise 2

Draw and label these pictures.

Choose two more words to draw and label.

## Exercise 3

Write these sentences, filling in the missing words.

**1** I _ _ _ _ _ _ things at the shop.
**2** I _ _ _ _ _ _ _ I knew the answer.
**3** _ _ _ _ _ _ is nothing.
**4** The boxers _ _ _ _ _ _ a good fight.
**5** Mother _ _ _ _ _ _ _ in the washing.

# are

hare

| | | |
|---|---|---|
| hare | spare | stare |
| rare | spared | stared |
| square | care | fare |
| dare | cared | welfare |
| dared | careful | declare |
| flare | careless | mare |
| flared | BEWARE | |

## Exercise 1

## Exercise 2

Write down all the **are** words you can see illustrated in this picture.

## Exercise 3

Write these sentences, filling in the missing words.

**1** A __ __ __ __ is an animal.
**2** __ __ __ __ __ __ __ means take care.
**3** A car has to have a __ __ __ __ __ wheel.
**4** A __ __ __ __ __ __ has four sides.
**5** We must pay a __ __ __ __ on the bus.

| | | |
|---|---|---|
| stew | drew | blew |
| few | crew | nephew |
| yew | screw | new |
| knew | threw | news |
| dew | Jew | newspaper |
| chew | jewel | view |
| grew | flew | ewe |

stew

# ew

## Exercise 1

## Exercise 2

Write down all the **ew** words you can see illustrated in this picture.

## Exercise 3

Write these sentences, filling in the missing words.

**1** The bird __ __ __ __ high up in the air.
**2** Many children like to __ __ __ __ gum.
**3** The men who work on a ship are called the __ __ __ __ .
**4** No-one __ __ __ __ the answer.
**5** A __ __ __ is a tree.

# ur

| | | | |
|---|---|---|---|
| church | turnip | murder | turning |
| churn | further | hurt | turned |
| purse | turbine | hurting | curl |
| nurse | purpose | hurtful | curly |
| turkey | purple | burn | curling |
| Thursday | Saturn | burning | curled |
| Saturday | burglar | burnt | hamburger |
| curtain | murmur | turn | beefburger |

## Exercise 1

## Exercise 2

Write down all the **ur** words you can see illustrated in this picture.

## Exercise 3

Write these sentences, filling in the missing words.

**1** A _ _ _ _ _ _ is a vegetable.
**2** A _ _ _ _ _ _ is a bird.
**3** A cut hand may _ _ _ _ .
**4** A _ _ _ _ _ _ _ hangs at a window.
**5** There is a planet called _ _ _ _ _ _ .

| | | |
|---|---|---|
| pearl | earnest | search |
| heard | earnestly | searcher |
| earl | learn | searching |
| early | learner | searched |
| earlier | learning | hearse |
| earliest | learned | earth |

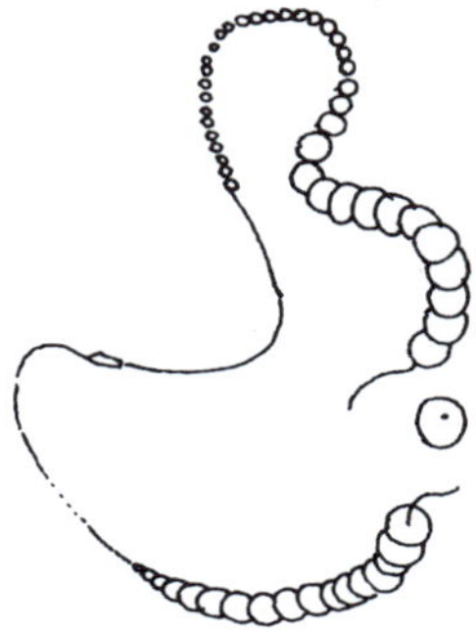

pearl

# ear

## Exercise 1

## Exercise 2

Write down all the **ear** words you can see illustrated in this picture.

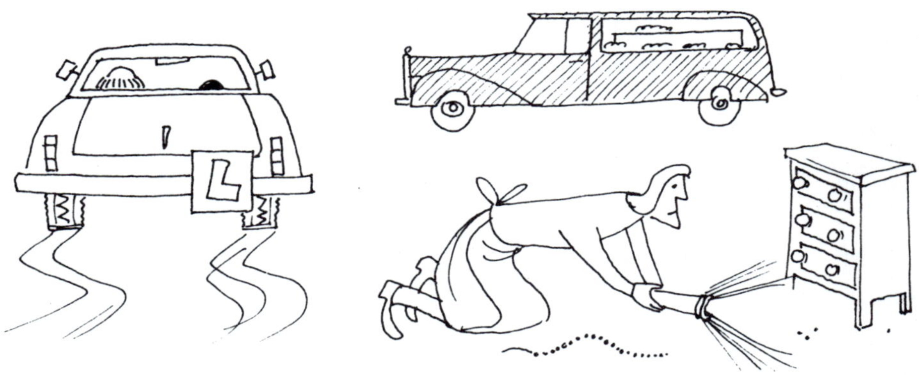

## Exercise 3

Write these sentences, filling in the missing words.

**1** We _ _ _ _ _ lessons at school.
**2** A _ _ _ _ _ is a jewel.
**3** Six o'clock in the morning is _ _ _ _ _ .
**4** Coffins are carried in a _ _ _ _ _ _ .
**5** Moles live in the _ _ _ _ _ .

# aw

paw

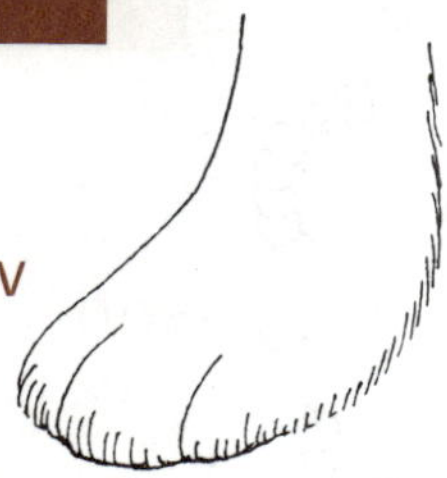

| | | | |
|---|---|---|---|
| paw | lawyer | pawn | draw |
| saw | law | hawk | drawer |
| raw | lawful | awkward | drawing |
| straw | dawn | jackdaw | drawn |
| jaw | yawn | shawl | |
| claw | yawning | prawn | |
| lawn | yawned | hawthorn | |

## Exercise 1

## Exercise 2

Write down all the **aw** words you can see illustrated in this picture.

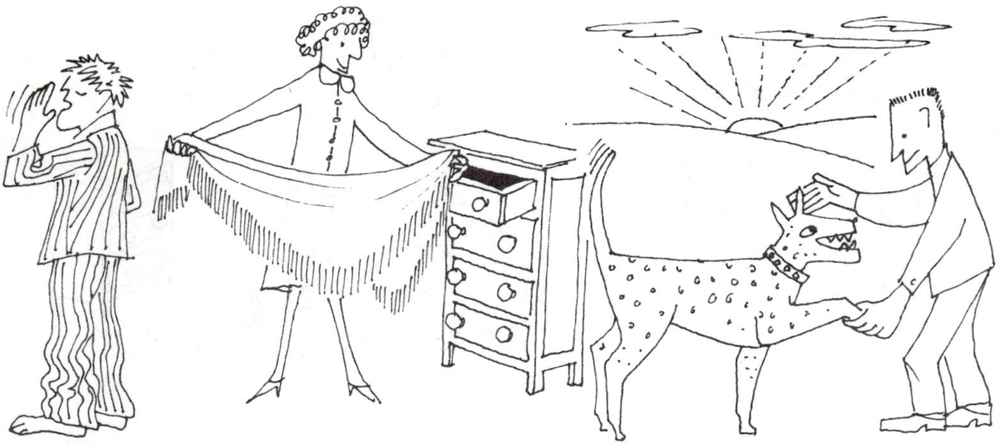

## Exercise 3

Write these sentences, filling in the missing words.

1 The _ _ _ _ and _ _ _ _ _ _ _ are birds.
2 A dog's foot is called a _ _ _ .
3 A bird's nail is called a _ _ _ _ .
4 We may _ _ _ _ when we are tired.
5 The sky gets light at _ _ _ _ .

| | | | |
|---|---|---|---|
| boy | toy | annoy | enjoy |
| boyish | Roy | annoyed | enjoyed |
| boyhood | royal | annoying | enjoying |
| joy | buoy | destroy | enjoyable |
| joyful | convoy | destroyed | destroyer |
| joyous | voyage | destroying | |

# oy

## Exercise 1

## Exercise 2

Write down all the **oy** words you can see illustrated in this picture.

## Exercise 3

Write these sentences, filling in the missing words.

**1** We play with a __ __ __ .
**2** A male child is called a __ __ __ .
**3** __ __ __ is a boy's name.
**4** We have fun when we __ __ __ __ __ ourselves.
**5** We may take a sea __ __ __ __ __ __ .

# oi

coin

| | | | |
|---|---|---|---|
| coin | boil | point | join |
| oil | boiler | pointed | joiner |
| soil | boiling | pointing | joining |
| foil | boiled | pointer | joined |
| voice | spoil | noise | joint |
| toilet | spoiling | noisy | |
| ointment | spoiled | noisier | |
| | | noisiest | choir |

## Exercise 1

## Exercise 2

Write down all the **oi** words you can see illustrated in this picture.

## Exercise 3

Write these sentences, filling in the missing words.

**1** A __ __ __ __ is a piece of money.
**2** Flowers grow in __ __ __ __ .
**3** We __ __ __ __ water for making tea.
**4** We use __ __ __ __ __ __ __ __ to soothe a sore.
**5** A __ __ __ __ __ __ makes things with wood.

# ie

| | | |
|---|---|---|
| shield | priest | relief |
| field | niece | relieve |
| piece | pier | belief |
| brief | reprieve | believe |
| thief | grief | |
| chief | grieve | friend |

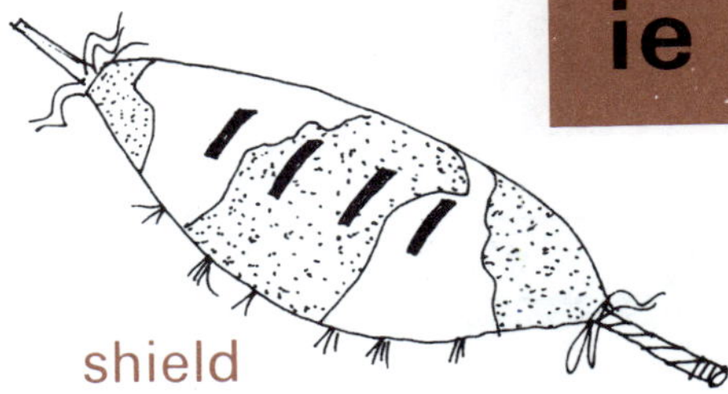

shield

## Exercise 1

## Exercise 2

Write down all the **ie** words you can see illustrated in this picture.

## Exercise 3

Write these sentences, filling in the missing words.

**1** We _ _ _ _ _ _ when we are sad.
**2** The cows ate the grass in the _ _ _ _ _.
**3** A _ _ _ _ _ steals things.
**4** My sister's daughter is my _ _ _ _ _.
**5** The boss of a tribe is called a _ _ _ _ _.

# cei

ceiling

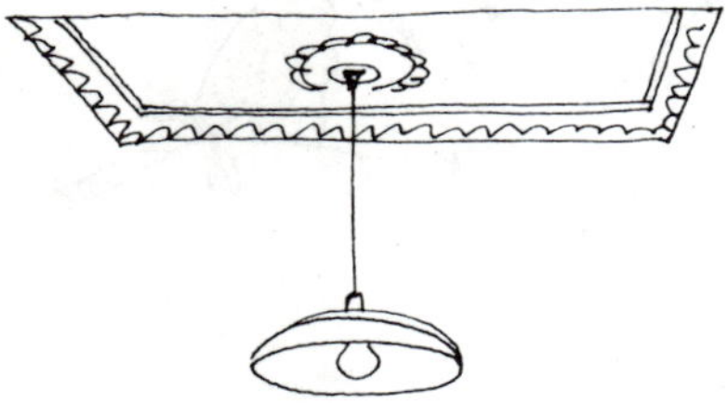

| | | |
|---|---|---|
| ceiling | perceive | conceit |
| receive | perceiving | conceited |
| receiving | perceived | |
| receiver | deceive | |
| received | deceiving | |
| receipt | deceived | |

## Exercise 1

## Exercise 2

Draw and label these pictures.

Choose two more words to draw and label.

## Exercise 3

Write these sentences, filling in the missing words.

1 The top of a room is called the _ _ _ _ _ _ _ .
2 A _ _ _ _ _ _ _ _ proves we have paid the bill.
3 A _ _ _ _ _ _ _ _ _ _ person is vain.
4 He did not _ _ _ _ _ _ _ _ the truth.
5 To _ _ _ _ _ _ _ _ is to hide the truth.

| | |
|---|---|
| seize<br>seized<br>seizure<br>weir<br>weird | heir |
| | either<br>neither |

**ei**

## Exercise 1

## Exercise 2

Draw and label these pictures.

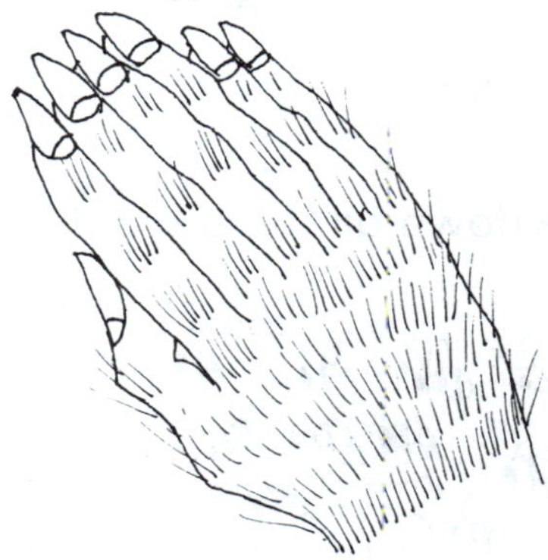

Choose one more word to draw and label.

## Exercise 3

Write these sentences, filling in the missing words.

**1** _ _ _ _ _ means very unusual.
**2** To _ _ _ _ _ is to grab.
**3** A _ _ _ _ is where water falls.
**4** He was _ _ _ _ _ _ _ rich nor poor.
**5** You can go _ _ _ _ _ _ up or down a staircase.

# o

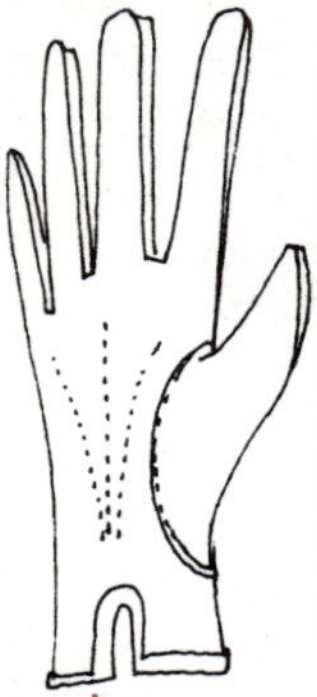

glove

| | | | | |
|---|---|---|---|---|
| glove | other | some | love | worry |
| son | mother | someone | lovely | worrier |
| ton | brother | somehow | lovelier | worried |
| done | another | something | loveliest | comfort |
| front | dozen | somewhere | won | comforting |
| sponge | above | somebody | wonder | comfortable |
| Monday | honey | come | wonderful | cover |
| London | money | coming | wonderfully | covered |
| shovel | monkey | month | colour | oven |
| | stomach | monthly | colourful | sloven |
| | | | coloured | slovenly |

## Exercise 1

## Exercise 2

Write down all the **o** words you can see illustrated in this picture.

## Exercise 3

Write these sentences, filling in the missing words.

**1** __ __ __ __ __ __ is the capital of England.
**2** There are twelve __ __ __ __ __ s in a year.
**3** When Bill was late home from school his father started to __ __ __ __ __ .
**4** A bee makes __ __ __ __ __ .
**5** Mother's boy is called her __ __ __ .

# ore

| | |
|---|---|
| core | wore |
| ore | swore |
| bore | gore |
| more | score |
| pore | store |
| tore | snore |
| lore | adore |
| fore | shore |
| before | ashore |

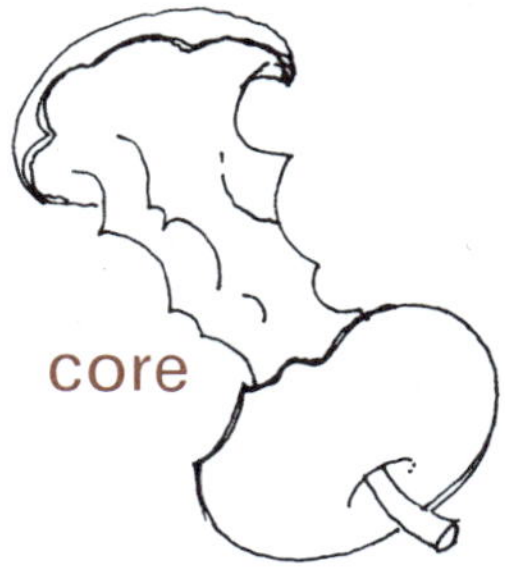


## Exercise 1

## Exercise 2

Write down all the **ore** words you can see illustrated in this picture.

## Exercise 3

Write these sentences, filling in the missing words.

**1** An apple has a __ __ __ __ in the middle.
**2** The __ __ __ __ __ is by the sea.
**3** Twenty is a __ __ __ __ __ .
**4** __ __ __ __ __ __ means in front of.
**5** Six is one __ __ __ __ than five.

# ey

key

key
donkey
monkey
hockey
turkey
money
chimney
valley
journey

## Exercise 1

## Exercise 2

Write down all the **ey** words you can see illustrated in this picture.

## Exercise 3

Write these sentences, filling in the missing words.

**1** We can ride a _ _ _ _ _ _ _ _ _ .
**2** Smoke comes from a _ _ _ _ _ _ _ _ _ _ .
**3** A _ _ _ unlocks a door.
**4** We spend _ _ _ _ _ _ _ .
**5** A _ _ _ _ _ _ _ _ and a _ _ _ _ _ _ _ _ are animals.

| | | |
|---|---|---|
| cough<br>trough | plough<br>bough | dough<br>though<br>although |
| thorough<br>thoroughly<br>borough | through | rough<br>tough<br>enough |

# ough

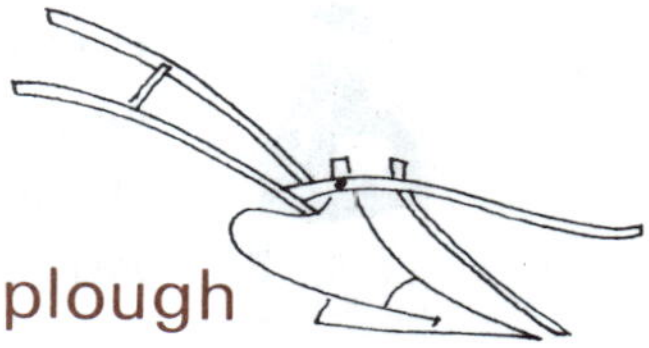

plough

## Exercise 1

## Exercise 2

Write down all the **ough** words you can see illustrated in this picture.

## Exercise 3

Write these sentences, filling in the missing words.

1 The strong boots were made of _ _ _ _ _ leather.
2 If we want our work to be perfect we must be
_ _ _ _ _ _ _ _ _ .
3 The farmer _ _ _ _ _ _ed his field.
4 A tickle in the throat can make you _ _ _ _ _ .
5 _ _ _ _ _ _ _ _ Jane is clever, she is lazy, so she does not do well at school.

# au

sauce

| | | | |
|---|---|---|---|
| sauce | haul | author | automatic |
| saucer | launch | auburn | astronaut |
| Paul | haunt | audience | plausible |
| Pauline | pause | laundry | caution |
| Maud | fault | applaud | cautious |
| Audrey | faulty | tarpaulin | cause |
| August | vault | (Santa) Claus | because |
| maul | autumn | | |

## Exercise 1

## Exercise 2

Write down all the **au** words you can see illustrated in this picture.

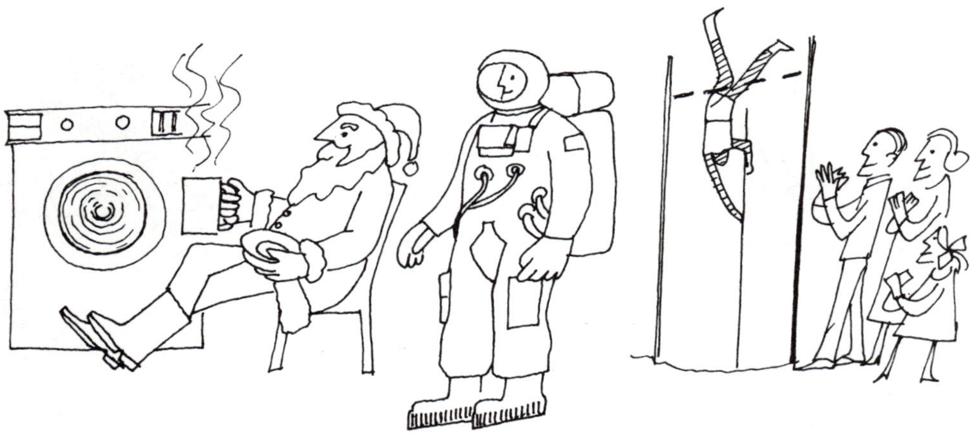

## Exercise 3

Write these sentences, filling in the missing words.

**1** A book is written by an _ _ _ _ _ _ .
**2** We use a cup and _ _ _ _ _ _ at tea time.
**3** Santa _ _ _ _ _ comes at Christmas.
**4** _ _ _ _ is a boy's and _ _ _ _ _ _ _ is a girl's name.

| | | |
|---|---|---|
| country | double | |
| young | trouble | |
| touch | nourish | |
| touching | nourishing | |
| touched | nourished | rough |
| couple | nourishment | tough |
| cousin | flourish | enough |

**ou**

country

## Exercise 1

## Exercise 2

Write down all the **ou** words you can see illustrated in this picture.

## Exercise 3

Write these sentences, filling in the missing words.

**1** We _ _ _ _ _ things with our hands.
**2** If we do wrong we may get into _ _ _ _ _ _ _ .
**3** Food gives us _ _ _ _ _ _ _ _ _ _ _ .
**4** Spain is a _ _ _ _ _ _ _ .
**5** My _ _ _ _ _ _ is my uncle's child.

# ei

| | | | |
|---|---|---|---|
| reindeer | sleigh | weigh | eight |
| rein | neigh | weighing | eighteen |
| reign | neighing | weighed | eighty |
| vein | neighed | weight | |
| | neighbour | freight | |

heir
their
leisure

height

reindeer

## Exercise 1

## Exercise 2

Write down all the **ei** words you can see illustrated in this picture.

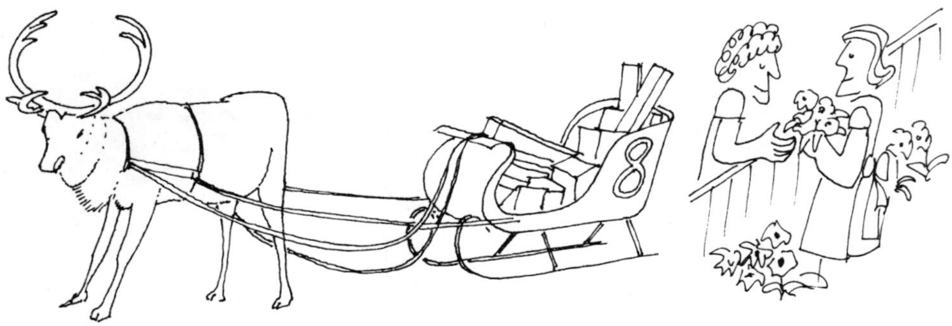

## Exercise 3

Write these sentences, filling in the missing words.

**1** The people who live next door are our _ _ _ _ _ _ _ _ _ s.
**2** A dog barks. A horse _ _ _ _ _ s.
**3** Blood runs in our _ _ _ _ s.
**4** The number after seventy-nine is _ _ _ _ _ _ .
**5** People should wash _ _ _ _ _ hands before they eat.

# war

war
ward
reward
forward
backward
wart
warm
warmth
warn
warning
warble
dwarf
swarm

## Exercise 1

## Exercise 2

Write down all the **war** words you can see illustrated in this picture.

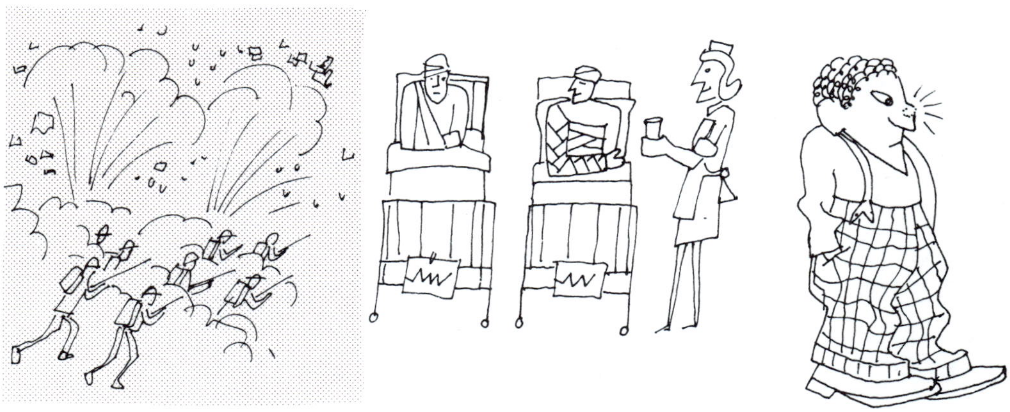

## Exercise 3

Write these sentences, filling in the missing words.

**1** A group of bees is called a _ _ _ _ _ .
**2** In hospital we sleep in a _ _ _ _ .
**3** Heating keeps us _ _ _ _ .
**4** He got a _ _ _ _ _ _ for finding the stolen property.
**5** People fight in a _ _ _ .

# quar

quartet

quartet
quarter
quart
quarto
quartz

## Exercise 1

## Exercise 2

Draw and label these pictures.

Choose one more word to draw and label.

## Exercise 3

Write these sentences, filling in the missing words.

**1** A fourth is a __ __ __ __ __ __ __ .
**2** Four people playing music together are a __ __ __ __ __ __ __ .
**3** __ __ __ __ __ __ is a rock.
**4** Two pints equal one __ __ __ __ __ .

**ar**

| | |
|---|---|
| Mary | parent |
| wary | library |
| area | librarian |
| daring | contrary |
| sharing | canary |
| scaring | scarce |
| paring | scarcely |

parent

## Exercise 1

## Exercise 2

Draw and label these pictures.

Choose two more words to draw and label.

## Exercise 3

Write these sentences, filling in the missing words.

1 We borrow books from a ________ .
2 ________ means a thing is hard to get.
3 ________ is a girl's name.
4 A ________ is a bird.
5 My mother is one of my ________ s.

# tion

invention

| | |
|---|---|
| invention | action |
| station | direction |
| nation | collection |
| destination | reflection |
| relation | condition |
| population | mention |
| attraction | position |

## Exercise 1

## Exercise 2

Write down all the **tion** words you can see illustrated in this picture.

## Exercise 3

Write these sentences, filling in the missing words.

**1** We see a __ __ __ __ __ __ __ __ __ __ in a mirror.
**2** London was the __ __ __ __ __ __ __ __ __ __ __ of the train.
**3** Britain is a __ __ __ __ __ __ .
**4** He caught his train at the __ __ __ __ __ __ __ .
**5** He travelled in a westerly __ __ __ __ __ __ __ __ __ .

| | |
|---|---|
| door<br>floor | moor<br>poor |

door

**oor**

## Exercise 1

## Exercise 2

Draw and label these pictures.

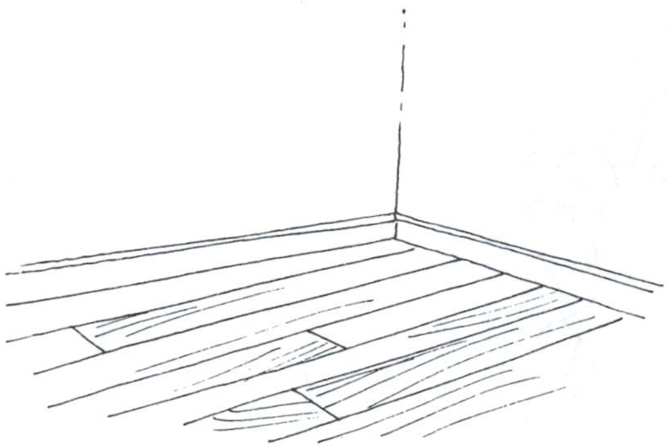

Choose two more words to draw and label.

## Exercise 3

Write these sentences, filling in the missing words.

1 I walk on the _ _ _ _ _ .
2 _ _ _ _ people have little money.
3 The sheep were on the _ _ _ _ .
4 You can open and shut a _ _ _ _ .

# ie

tie
die
lie
pie

## Exercise 1 

## Exercise 2

Draw and label these pictures.

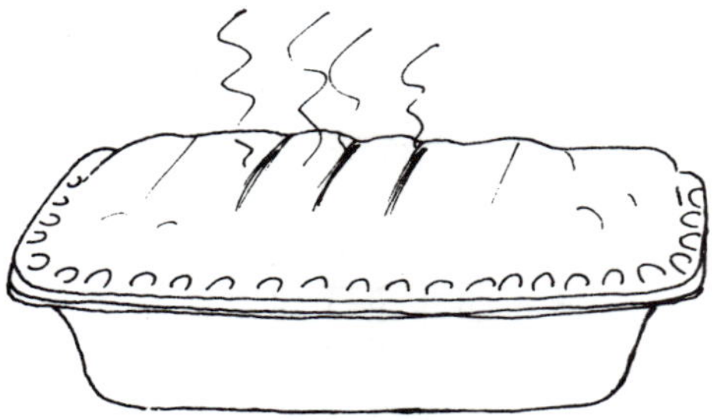

Choose two more words to draw and label.

## Exercise 3

Write these sentences, filling in the missing words.

**1** Mother baked an apple __ __ __ .
**2** In a war many men are killed and __ __ __ .
**3** We __ __ __ a knot.
**4** I __ __ __ my head on a pillow.

# ue

| | |
|---|---|
| glue | sue |
| blue | issue |
| clue | value |
| true | |

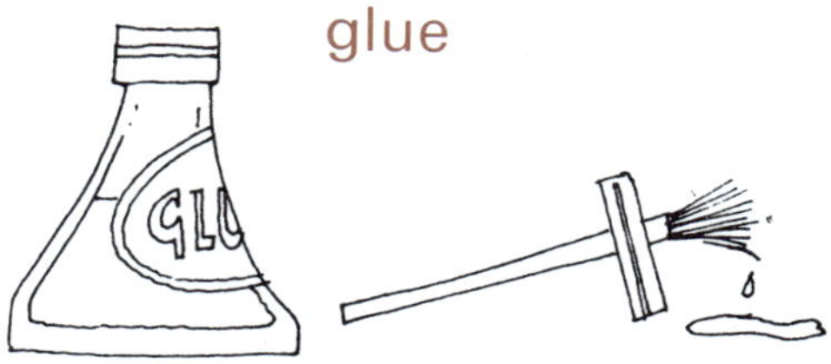

glue

## Exercise 1

## Exercise 2

Draw and label these pictures.

Choose two more words to draw and label.

## Exercise 3

Write these sentences, filling in the missing words.

**1** _ _ _ _ is a colour.
**2** We stick things with _ _ _ _ .
**3** Something of _ _ _ _ _ is worth a lot of money.
**4** It is honest to give a _ _ _ _ answer.
**5** If we want to solve a problem we look for a _ _ _ _ .

# oe

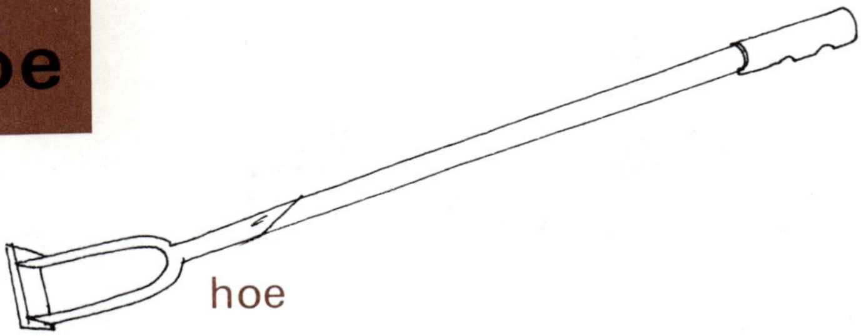


| | |
|---|---|
| hoe<br>toe<br>doe<br>foe | shoe |

## Exercise 1

## Exercise 2

Draw and label these pictures.

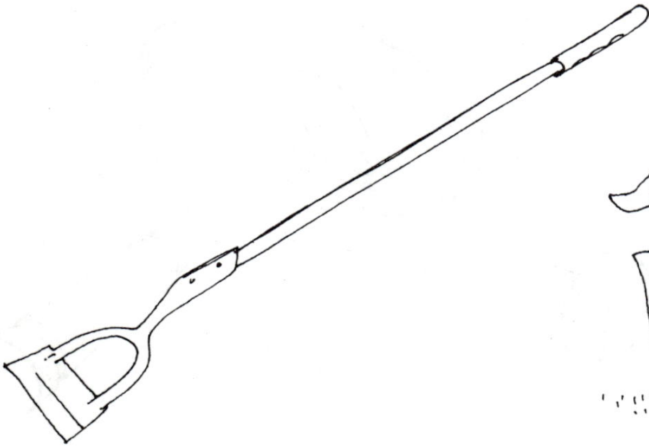

Choose two more words to draw and label.

## Exercise 3

Write these sentences, filling in the missing words.

**1** We weed the garden with a __ __ __ .
**2** A __ __ __ is an enemy.
**3** A __ __ __ is a female deer.
**4** I have five __ __ __ s on each foot.
**5** I wear a __ __ __ __ on each foot.

wound
coupon
you
soup
group

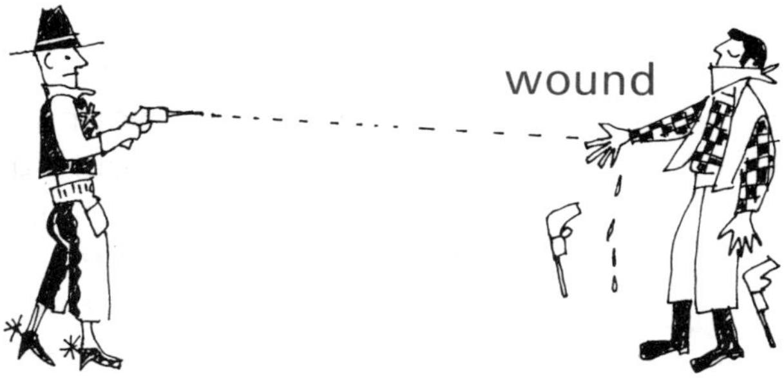


**ou**

## Exercise 1

## Exercise 2

Draw and label these pictures.

Choose two more words to draw and label.

## Exercise 3

Write these sentences, filling in the missing words.

**1** My dad fills in his football pools __ __ __ __ __ __ .
**2** We may start dinner with __ __ __ __ .
**3** Several people are called a __ __ __ __ __ .
**4** __ __ __ have your own things.
**5** A __ __ __ __ __ will need to be treated.

# our

pour
pouring
poured
four
fourteen
fourteenth
resource
resourceful
your
yours
yourself
favour
favourite
source
honour

## Exercise 1

## Exercise 2

Draw and label these pictures.

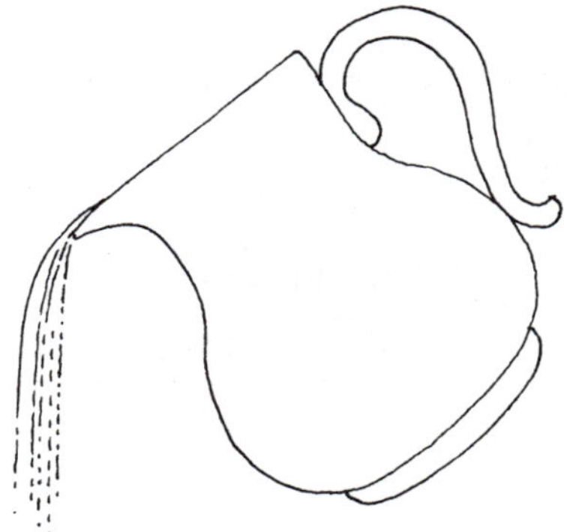

Choose two more words to draw and label.

## Exercise 3

Write these sentences, filling in the missing words.

1 _ _ _ _ _ _ _ _ _ comes before fifteen.
2 _ _ _ _ property belongs to you.
3 _ _ _ _ comes after three.
4 We _ _ _ _ liquid.
5 We like our _ _ _ _ _ _ _ _ _ things best.

fruit
bruise
cruise
juice
suit
suitable
unsuitable

ui

## Exercise 1

## Exercise 2

Write down all the **ui** words you can see illustrated in this picture.

## Exercise 3

Write these sentences, filling in the missing words.

**1** An apple is a _ _ _ _ _ .
**2** We may _ _ _ _ _ _ in a ship.
**3** A _ _ _ _ may have a jacket and trousers.
**4** We squeeze an orange to get the _ _ _ _ _ .
**5** A knock on the arm may cause a _ _ _ _ _ _ .

# oar

oar

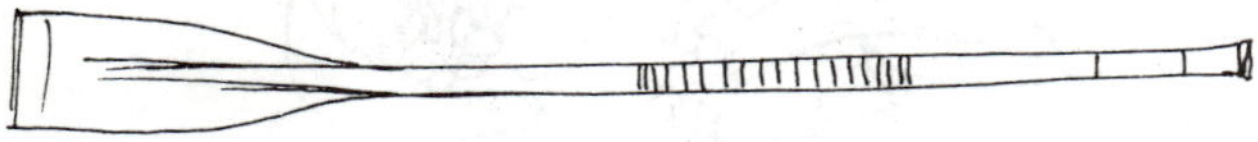

| | |
|---|---|
| oar | soar |
| boar | soaring |
| coarse | soared |
| hoarse | board |
| roar | cupboard |
| roaring | aboard |
| roared | overboard |

## Exercise 1

## Exercise 2

Write down all the **oar** words you can see illustrated in this picture.

## Exercise 3

Write these sentences, filling in the missing words.

**1** We row a boat with __ __ __ s.
**2** We can store things in a __ __ __ __ __ __ __ __ .
**3** A lion __ __ __ __ s.
**4** A __ __ __ __ is an animal.
**5** The bird __ __ __ __ __ __ up into the sky.

# al

palm
half
calf
calm
psalm
almond

palm

## Exercise 1

## Exercise 2

Write down all the **al** words you can see illustrated in this picture.

## Exercise 3

Write these sentences, filling in the missing words.

**1** A _ _ _ _ is a baby cow.
**2** Thirty minutes is _ _ _ _ an hour.
**3** A _ _ _ _ sea is smooth.
**4** _ _ _ _ _ _ s are nuts.
**5** The _ _ _ _ is part of the hand.

# alk

walk

walk
talk
chalk
stalk

## Exercise 1

## Exercise 2

Draw and label these pictures.

Choose two more words to draw and label.

## Exercise 3

Write these sentences, filling in the missing words.

1 We _ _ _ _ with our legs.
2 We _ _ _ _ with our voices.
3 _ _ _ _ _ is used to write on a blackboard.
4 A flower has a _ _ _ _ _ .

# aught

| | |
|---|---|
| caught | slaughter |
| taught | daughter |
| naughty | |
| laugh | laughed |
| laughing | laughter |

slaughter

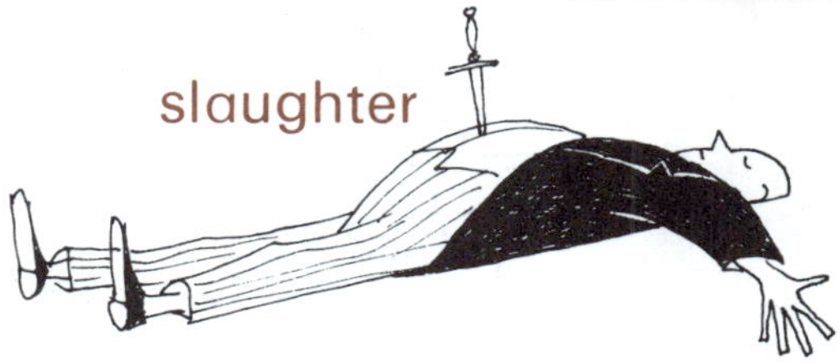

## Exercise 1

## Exercise 2

Write down all the **aught** words you can see illustrated in this picture.

## Exercise 3

Write these sentences, filling in the missing words.

**1** The teacher _ _ _ _ _ _ _ the children.
**2** The fisherman _ _ _ _ _ _ _ some fish.
**3** We _ _ _ _ _ _ _ _ _ _ animals for food.
**4** A girl child is called a _ _ _ _ _ _ _ _ _ .
**5** It is _ _ _ _ _ _ _ _ to disobey.

# oul

soul
shoulder
smoulder
boulder
mould
mouldy

## Exercise 1

## Exercise 2

Draw and label these pictures.

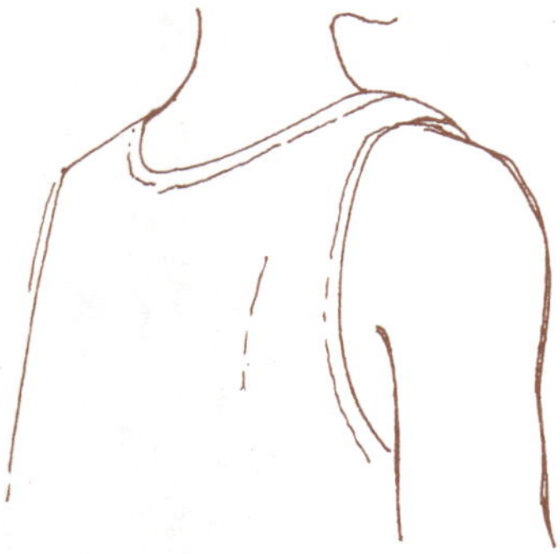

Choose one more word to draw and label.

## Exercise 3

Write these sentences, filling in the missing words.

**1** A _ _ _ _ _ _ _ _ is a big rock.
**2** The _ _ _ _ _ _ _ _ _ is at the top of the arm.
**3** SOS means 'Save our _ _ _ _ s.'
**4** A dying fire may _ _ _ _ _ _ _ _ _ .
**5** The stale bread was _ _ _ _ _ _ .

| | |
|---|---|
| sugar | usual |
| sure | usually |
| surely | unusual |
| measure | unusually |
| treasure | |
| pleasure | |

**su**

sugar

## Exercise 1

## Exercise 2

Draw and label these pictures.

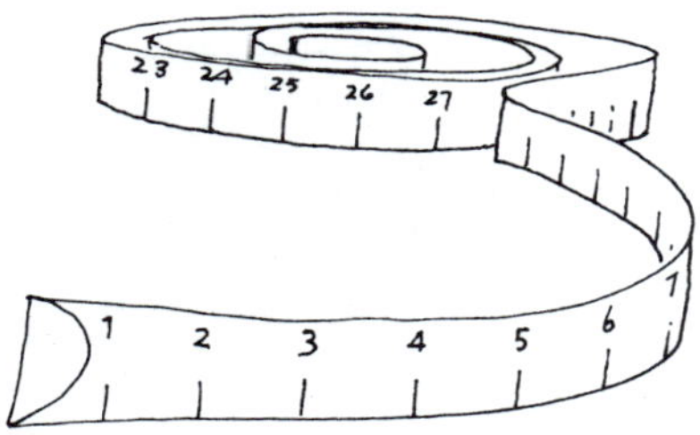


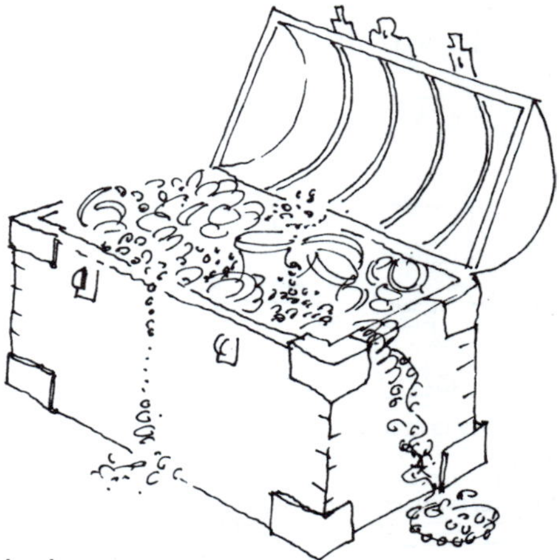

Choose one more word to draw and label.

## Exercise 3

Write these sentences, filling in the missing words.

1 _ _ _ _ _ is sweet.
2 We _ _ _ _ _ _ _ with a ruler.
3 We get _ _ _ _ _ _ _ _ from doing nice things.
4 Certain means _ _ _ _ .
5 Married women _ _ _ _ _ _ _ wear a wedding ring.

# y

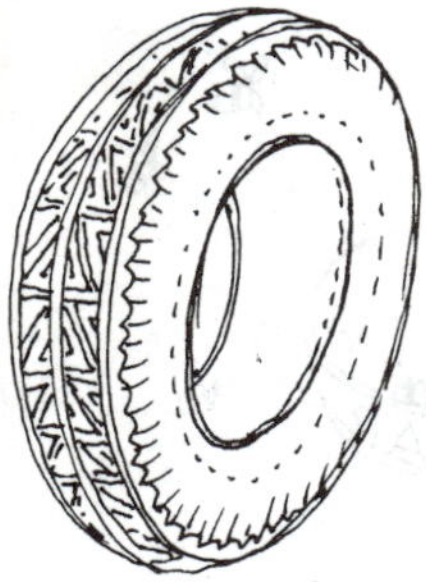

tyre

| | | |
|---|---|---|
| tyre | hyacinth | cyclone |
| type | nylon | dynamo |
| style | pylon | dynamic |
| byre | xylophone | dynamite |
| gyrate | cycle | dyke |
| hydro | typhoon | python |
| hydrant | | |
| hydrangea | | |

## Exercise 1

## Exercise 2

Write down all the **y** words you can see illustrated in this picture.

## Exercise 3

Write these sentences, filling in the missing words.

**1** I can ride a _ _ _ _ _ .
**2** A _ _ _ _ _ _ is a snake.
**3** Cows may live in a _ _ _ _ .
**4** _ _ _ _ _ _ _ _ blows things up.
**5** Strong winds blow in a _ _ _ _ _ _ _ .

## y

| | | | |
|---|---|---|---|
| syringe | physical | sympathy | cynic |
| syrup | dynasty | symptom | gym |
| system | dysentery | symmetry | gymnasium |
| systematic | lymph | symphony | mystery |
| hymn | pyramid | symbol | mysterious |
| rhythm | sycamore | cylinder | myth |
| physics | synagogue | cymbal | bicycle |

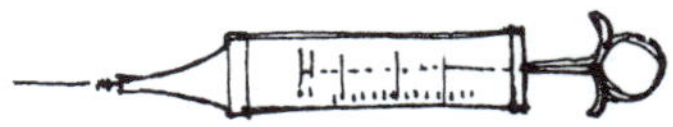

syringe

## Exercise 1

## Exercise 2

Write down all the **y** words you can see illustrated in this picture.

## Exercise 3

Write these sentences, filling in the missing words.

1 ______________ is sweet.
2 At church we sing ____________s.
3 A ________________________ is a tree.
4 We study ______________________ at school.
5 Something we cannot solve is called a ____________________.

## qu

queen

| | | |
|---|---|---|
| queen | quite | squirt |
| quack | quiet | enquire |
| quick | quench | require |
| quill | squeak | squirrel |
| quilt | squeaky | liquid |
| quiver | squeeze | |
| queer | squeal | |

### Exercise 1

### Exercise 2

Write down all the **qu** words you can see illustrated in this picture.

### Exercise 3

Write these sentences, filling in the missing words.

1 Water is a _ _ _ _ _ _ .
2 A duck's sound is called a _ _ _ _ _ .
3 It is very _ _ _ _ _ when there is no sound.
4 A drink will _ _ _ _ _ _ your thirst.
5 _ _ _ _ _ means fast.

# silent letters

| | |
|---|---|
| bouquet | autumn |
| racquet | solemn |
| listen | receipt |
| sword | |
| tongue | |
| pneumatic | |
| pneumonia | |

bouquet

## Exercise 1

## Exercise 2

Write down all the words with **silent letters** you can see illustrated in this picture.

## Exercise 3

Write these sentences, filling in the missing words.

**1** She played tennis with a __ __ __ __ __ __ __ .
**2** A bicycle has __ __ __ __ __ __ __ __ __ tyres.
**3** The season after summer is __ __ __ __ __ __ .
**4** We __ __ __ __ __ __ if we want to hear something.
**5** The queen uses a __ __ __ __ __ when she knights people.

# Part II—patterns with consonants

## silent b

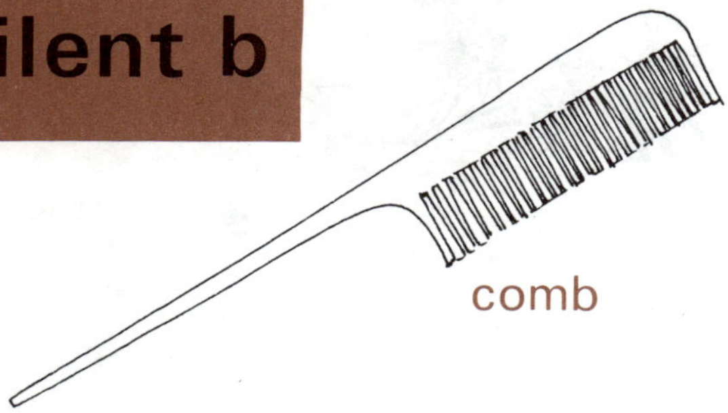


| | |
|---|---|
| comb | thumb |
| lamb | bomb |
| numb | climb |
| dumb | tomb |
| crumb | limb |
| plumb | debt |
| plumber | doubt |

### Exercise 1

### Exercise 2

Write down all the **silent b** words you can see illustrated in this picture.

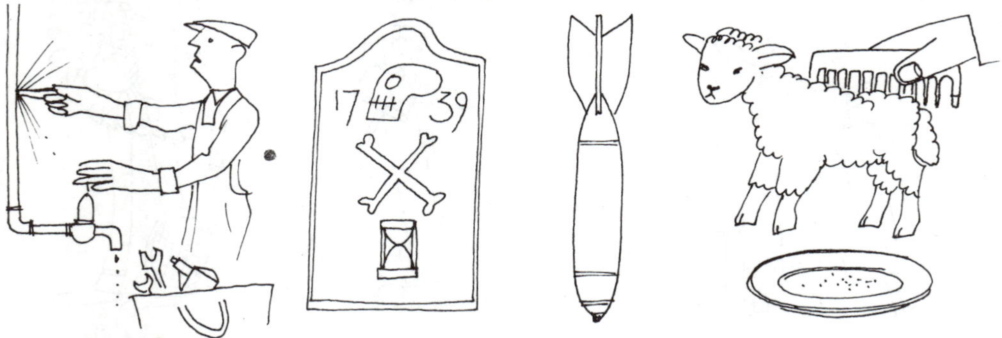


### Exercise 3

Write these sentences, filling in the missing words.

**1** We ________ our hair.
**2** A baby sheep is called a ________ .
**3** A ________ mends pipes.
**4** I have a ________ on each hand.
**5** If we owe money we are in ________ .

# bl

| | | |
|---|---|---|
| blossom | blacksmith | blush |
| blot | blister | blade |
| block | blink | blaze |
| blind | bleat | blazer |
| blank | bleed | blame |
| blanket | blood | blonde |
| black | blunt | bleach |

## Exercise 1

## Exercise 2

Write down all the **bl** words you can see illustrated in this picture.

## Exercise 3

Write these sentences, filling in the missing words.

**1** We put a _ _ _ _ _ _ _ on the bed.
**2** Sheep _ _ _ _ _ .
**3** A person who cannot see is _ _ _ _ _ .
**4** We may _ _ _ _ _ if we cut ourselves.
**5** _ _ _ _ _ is the opposite of white.

# br

brush

| | | |
|---|---|---|
| brush | brim | brass |
| brow | bring | brandy |
| brown | brick | branch |
| broom | brigade | bracket |
| brook | brake | bread |
| broke | brave | breeze |
| broken | bride | |

## Exercise 1

## Exercise 2

Write down all the **br** words you can see illustrated in this picture.

## Exercise 3

Write these sentences, filling in the missing words.

**1** ___ ___ ___ ___ ___ is a colour.
**2** I ___ ___ ___ ___ ___ the cup when I dropped it.
**3** ___ ___ ___ ___ ___ ___ is a drink.
**4** Many houses are built with ___ ___ ___ ___ ___ s.
**5** A ___ ___ ___ ___ ___ is a small stream.

## ch

| | | |
|---|---|---|
| cheese | check | chin |
| cheek | choose | cheap |
| child | chance | chart |
| children | chase | church |
| chest | chain | |
| chestnut | change | |
| cherry | chip | |

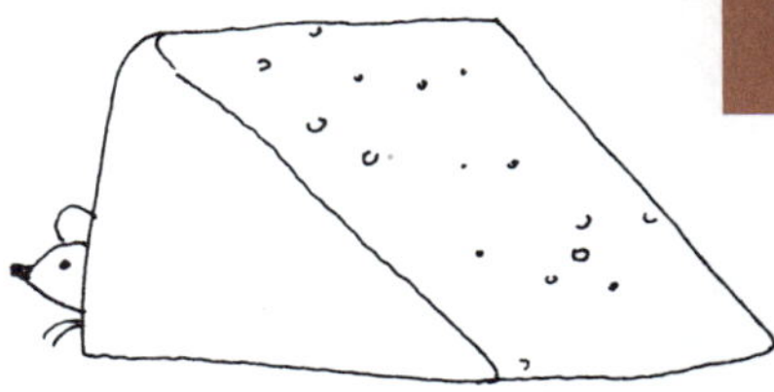

cheese

## Exercise 1

## Exercise 2

Write down all the **ch** words you can see illustrated in this picture.

## Exercise 3

Write these sentences, filling in the missing words.

**1** A __ __ __ __ __ __ is a fruit.
**2** A __ __ __ __ __ thing does not cost much.
**3** A __ __ __ __ __ is a young person.
**4** __ __ __ __ __ __ is made from milk.
**5** A __ __ __ __ __ has links.

# ch

| | | |
|---|---|---|
| chemist | chorus | chronicle |
| chord | character | scheme |
| chaos | characteristic | scholar |
| chasm | chromium | schooner |
| choir | cholera | ache |
| Christ | chronic | stomach |
| Christmas | chloroform | mechanic |
| chrysanthemum | Christopher | orchestra |
| technical | Michael | echo |
| architect | sepulchre | hypochondria |

chemist

## Exercise 1

## Exercise 2

Write down all the **ch** words you can see illustrated in this picture.

## Exercise 3

Write these sentences, filling in the missing words.

**1** 25 December is _ _ _ _ _ _ _ _ _ _ day.
**2** I took an aspirin for my head_ _ _ _ .
**3** The _ _ _ _ _ _ _ _ _ played a tune.
**4** _ _ _ _ _ _ _ _ is a disease.
**5** A sound that bounces back is called an _ _ _ _ .

## ck

| | | |
|---|---|---|
| duck | crack | trick |
| luck | pack | kick |
| suck | packet | chicken |
| stuck | neck | pick |
| truck | deck | prick |
| struck | wreck | lick |
| back | Dick | cock |
| sack | sick | sock |
| Jack | stick | rock |

duck

### Exercise 1

### Exercise 2

Write down all the **ck** words you can see illustrated in this picture.

### Exercise 3

Write these sentences, filling in the missing words.

**1** We _ _ _ _ a football.
**2** A _ _ _ _ can swim.
**3** _ _ _ _ and _ _ _ _ are boys' names.
**4** We _ _ _ _ a lollipop.

# cl

| | | |
|---|---|---|
| cliff | clash | clear |
| click | club | cloud |
| cling | clumsy | clue |
| clip | clutch | clever |
| clap | close | clock |
| class | clean | |

## Exercise 1

## Exercise 2

Write down all the **cl** words you can see illustrated in this picture.

## Exercise 3

Write these sentences, filling in the missing words.

**1** We ___ ___ ___ ___ our hands when we applaud.
**2** The ___ ___ ___ ___ ___ ___ boy kept tripping over things.
**3** A ___ ___ ___ ___ ___ tells us the time.
**4** Rain comes from ___ ___ ___ ___ ___s.
**5** The ___ ___ ___ ___ ___ ___ boy got all his sums right.

# cr

| | |
|---|---|
| crisp | crunch |
| crab | crust |
| crack | crutch |
| crash | cross |
| creep | crooked |
| cream | crimson |
| creak | crumb |

crisp

## Exercise 1

## Exercise 2

Write down all the **cr** words you can see illustrated in this picture.

## Exercise 3

Write these sentences, filling in the missing words.

1 ____________ is a colour.
2 A ________ is a sea creature.
3 The crispy edge of bread is called the ________ .
4 ____________ means twisted.
5 Angry means ________ .

# dr

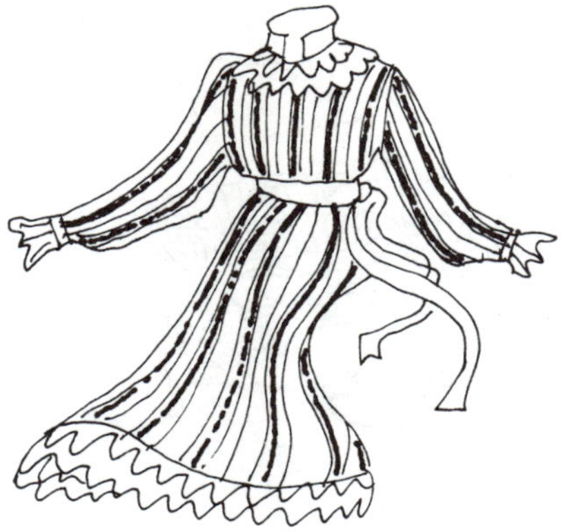

dress

dress
drive
driver
drink
drip
draw
drag
dragon
dream
drain
drove
drop
drum
drunk
drank

## Exercise 1

## Exercise 2

Write down all the **dr** words you can see illustrated in this picture.

## Exercise 3

Write these sentences, filling in the missing words.

**1** A _ _ _ _ _ _ _ is a creature in fairy tales.
**2** We _ _ _ _ a picture.
**3** A _ _ _ _ _ is a frock.
**4** He _ _ _ _ _ his milk.
**5** I _ _ _ _ _ the car.

toffee
coffee
off
stiff
sniff
cuff
puff
stuff

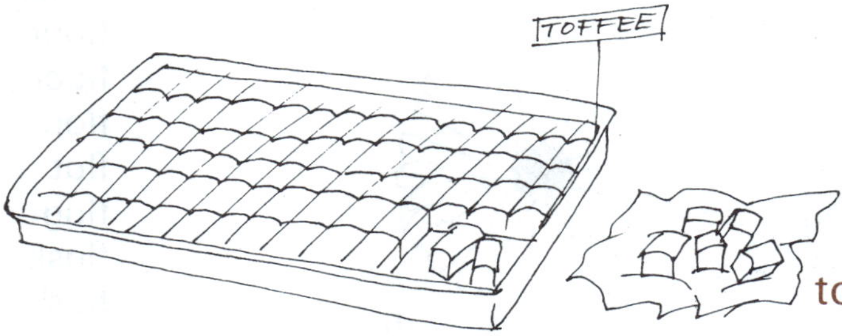

toffee

# ff

## Exercise 1

## Exercise 2

Write down all the **ff** words you can see illustrated in this picture.

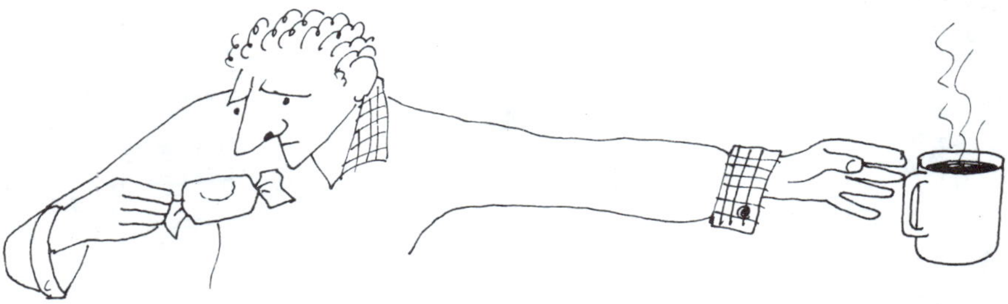

## Exercise 3

Write these sentences, filling in the missing words.

**1** A _ _ _ _ _ _ _ is a sweet.
**2** We drink _ _ _ _ _ _ _ .
**3** Starch makes things _ _ _ _ _ .
**4** He fell _ _ _ the seat.
**5** We _ _ _ _ _ with our noses.

# fl

flower

| | |
|---|---|
| flower | flake |
| flour | flame |
| flock | floor |
| flop | fly |
| flat | fleet |
| flag | fluff |
| flask | flush |
| flash | flutter |

## Exercise 1

## Exercise 2

Write down all the **fl** words you can see illustrated in this picture.

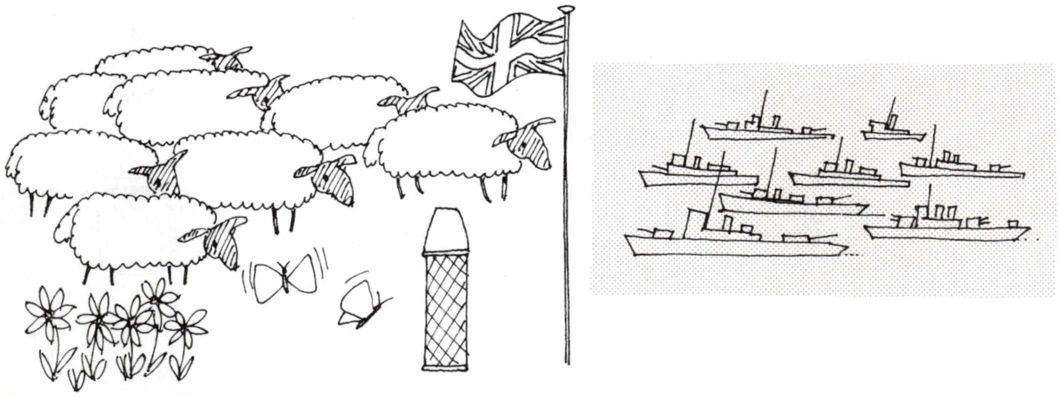

## Exercise 3

Write these sentences, filling in the missing words.

**1** A __ __ __ is an insect.
**2** We bake with __ __ __ __ __ .
**3** The shepherd has a __ __ __ __ __ of sheep.
**4** A rose is a __ __ __ __ __ __ .
**5** A fire has __ __ __ __ __s.

# fr

| | |
|---|---|
| frog | frame |
| frock | front |
| frost | from |
| free | freeze |
| fresh | |

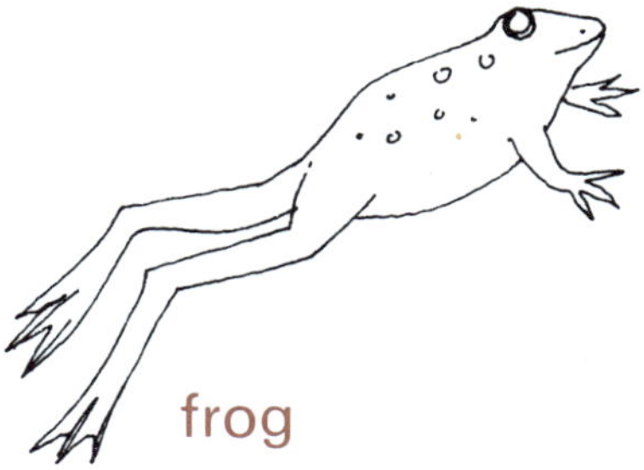

frog

## Exercise 1

## Exercise 2

Write down all the **fr** words you can see illustrated in this picture.

## Exercise 3

Write these sentences, filling in the missing words.

**1** Something which is __ __ __ __ costs nothing.
**2** A __ __ __ __ __ is a dress.
**3** A __ __ __ __ is an animal.
**4** Water __ __ __ __ __ __s to form ice.
**5** We put a picture in a __ __ __ __ __ .

# gl

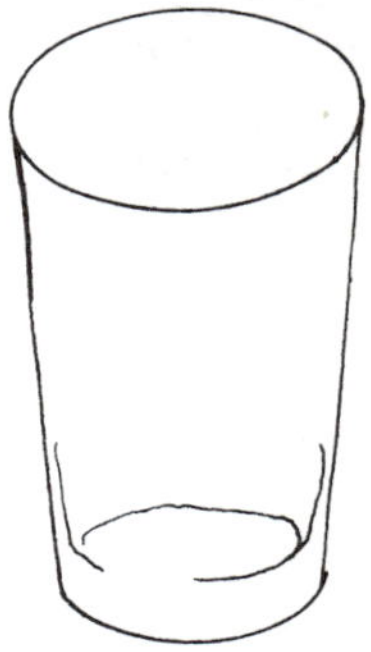

glass

| | | |
|---|---|---|
| glass | gloom | glade |
| glad | gleam | glance |
| glide | glee | gland |
| glider | glitter | glare |
| glow | glen | glaze |
| glossy | glory | glimpse |
| glue | glorious | glint |
| globe | glove | |

## Exercise 1

## Exercise 2

Write down all the **gl** words you can see illustrated in this picture.

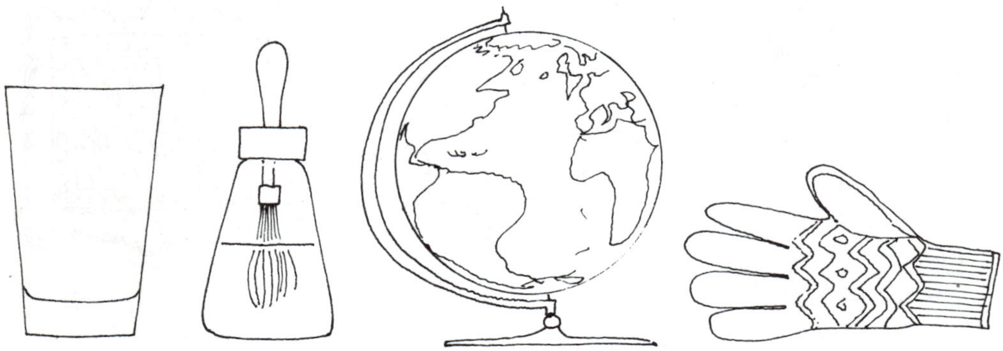

## Exercise 3

Write these sentences, filling in the missing words.

1 A __ __ __ __ __ __ can fly without an engine.
2 Pleased means __ __ __ __ .
3 __ __ __ __ __ __ is another word for shiny.
4 We drink from a __ __ __ __ __ .
5 We stick things with __ __ __ __ .

| | |
|---|---|
| gnome | sign |
| gnaw | design |
| gnat | resign |
| gnarled | ensign |
| gnu | consign |
| | reign |
| | campaign |

gnome

**gn**

## Exercise 1

## Exercise 2

Draw and label these pictures.

Choose two more words to draw and label.

## Exercise 3

Write these sentences, filling in the missing words.

**1** A ___ ___ ___ ___ post tells us the way.
**2** A ___ ___ ___ ___ ___ is a dwarf.
**3** A rat ___ ___ ___ ___s through things.
**4** A ___ ___ ___ ___ is an insect.
**5** A queen ___ ___ ___ ___ ___s.

# gr

grapes

| | | |
|---|---|---|
| grapes | gravel | greedy |
| grave | grit | green |
| grass | grip | gruff |
| grand | grin | grunt |
| grab | growl | grumble |
| grasp | ground | |

## Exercise 1

## Exercise 2

Write down all the **gr** words you can see illustrated in this picture.

## Exercise 3

Write these sentences, filling in the missing words.

**1** A person is buried under _ _ _ _ _ _ in a _ _ _ _ _ .
**3** The colour of grass is _ _ _ _ _ .
**3** _ _ _ _ _ _ are a fruit.
**4** To _ _ _ _ is to snatch.

ghost
rhyme
rhythm
rhubarb
John
rhinoceros
hour
honest
honour
dinghy

ghost

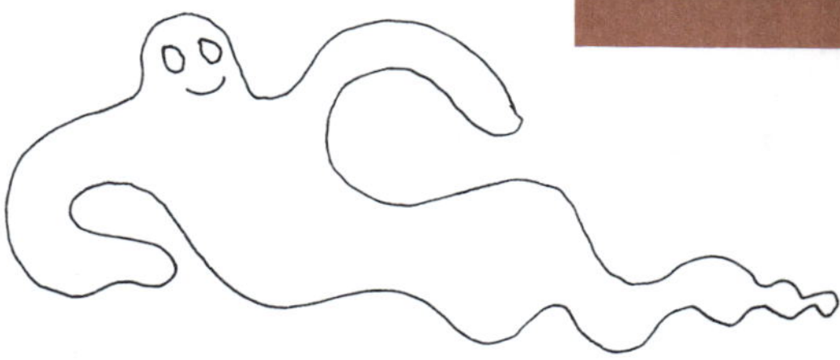

# silent h

## Exercise 1

## Exercise 2

Draw and label these pictures.

Choose two more words to draw and label.

## Exercise 3

Write these sentences, filling in the missing words.

1 _ _ _ _ _ _ _ is a fruit.
2 We can sail in a _ _ _ _ _ _ .
3 A _ _ _ _ _ _ _ _ _ _ is an animal.
4 It is _ _ _ _ _ _ to tell the truth.
5 _ _ _ _ is a boy's name.

# kn

knife
knight
know
knot
knob
knew
knee
kneel
knuckle

## Exercise 1

## Exercise 2

Write down all the **kn** words you can see illustrated in this picture.

## Exercise 3

Write these sentences, filling in the missing words.

**1** Nobody _ _ _ _ the right answer.
**2** I can bend my leg at the _ _ _ _ .
**3** We eat with a _ _ _ _ _ and fork.
**4** I can bend my finger at the _ _ _ _ _ _ _ .
**5** We tie a _ _ _ _ .

# mp

stamp
camp
damp
lamp
tramp
shampoo
hamper
imp
limp
pimple
lump
jump
jumper
pump
hump
bump
mumps
empty

stamp

## Exercise 1

## Exercise 2

Write down all the **mp** words you can see illustrated in this picture.

## Exercise 3

Write these sentences, filling in the missing words.

**1** We wash our hair with _ _ _ _ _ _ _ .
**2** I _ _ _ _ up my bicycle tyre.
**3** If one leg is sore we may _ _ _ _ .
**4** A _ _ _ _ gives light.
**5** We wear a _ _ _ _ _ _ .

# nd

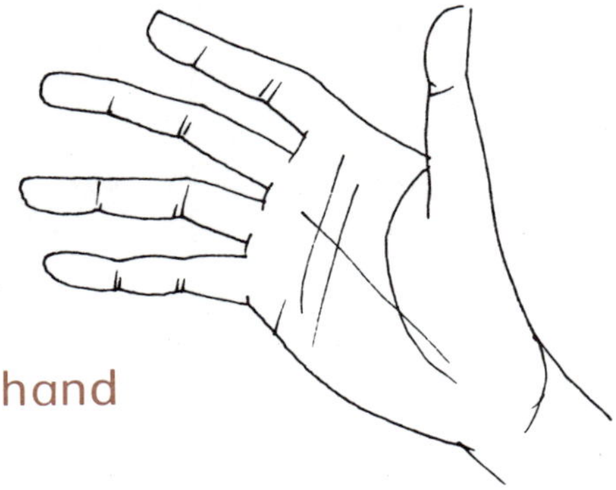

hand

| | |
|---|---|
| hand | pond |
| and | fund |
| band | end |
| land | mend |
| sand | send |
| stand | bend |
| errand | lend |
| wind | spend |

## Exercise 1

## Exercise 2

Write down all the **nd** words you can see illustrated in this picture.

## Exercise 3

Write these sentences, filling in the missing words.

**1** We __ __ __ __ __ on our feet.
**2** We __ __ __ __ __ money.
**3** My __ __ __ __ has five fingers.
**4** The __ __ __ __ played a tune.
**5** The __ __ __ __ blows.

| | | |
|---|---|---|
| ink | sank | trunk |
| wink | plank | sunk |
| sink | spank | bunk |
| stink | bank | shrunk |
| pink | tank | shrink |
| link | tanker | sprinkle |
| think | ankle | |

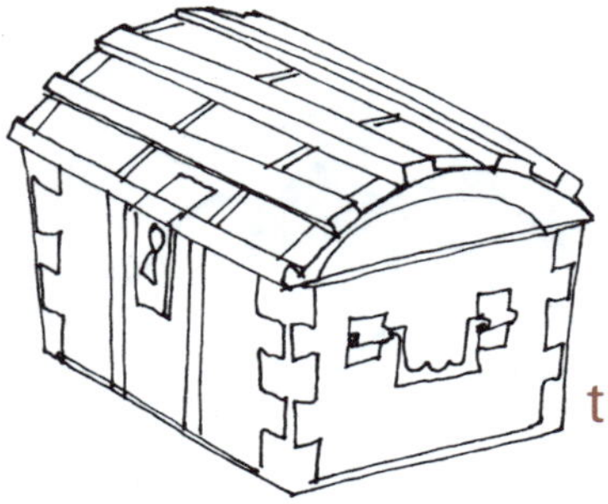

trunk

# nk

## Exercise 1

## Exercise 2

Write down all the **nk** words you can see illustrated in this picture.

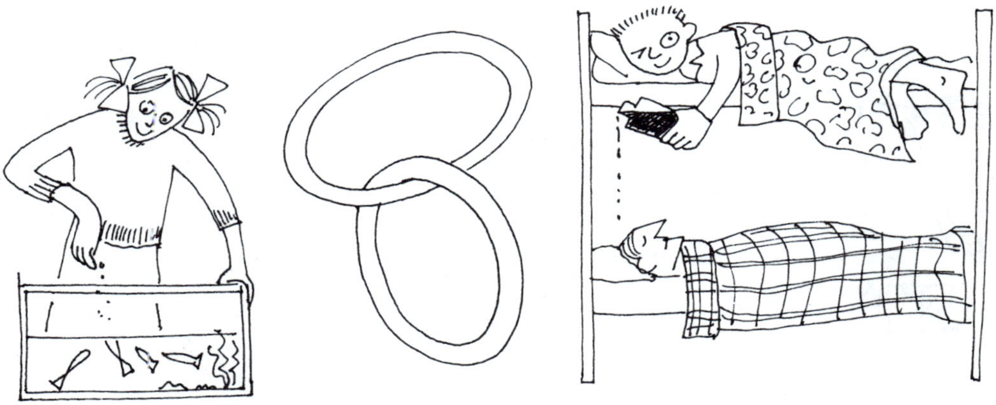

## Exercise 3

Write these sentences, filling in the missing words.

**1** _ _ _ _ is a colour.
**2** We _ _ _ _ with one eyelid.
**3** We may sleep in a _ _ _ _ bed.
**4** To _ _ _ _ _ is to smack.
**5** We wash dishes in a _ _ _ _ .

# nt

ant

| | | |
|---|---|---|
| ant | lent | winter |
| pant | rent | print |
| lantern | tent | grunt |
| bent | mint | hunt |
| went | splint | blunt |
| sent | splinter | shunt |
| spent | | |

## Exercise 1

## Exercise 2

Write down all the **nt** words you can see illustrated in this picture.

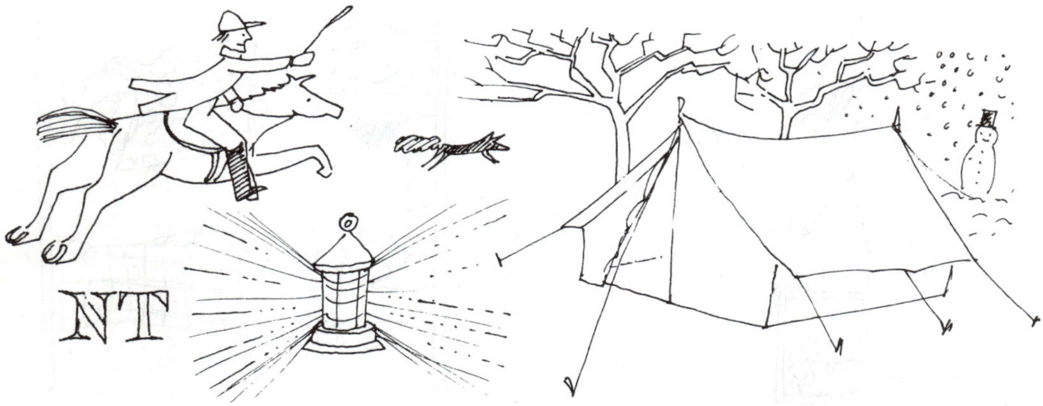


## Exercise 3

Write these sentences, filling in the missing words.

**1** Mother _ _ _ _ her child to school.
**2** I _ _ _ _ _ too much money.
**3** An _ _ _ is an insect.
**4** We sleep in a _ _ _ _ at camp.
**5** It is cold in _ _ _ _ _ _ .

| | | |
|---|---|---|
| phone | elephant | orphan |
| Philip | prophet | alphabet |
| phrase | prophecy | triumph |
| pheasant | nephew | Joseph |
| physics | graph | Stephen |
| photograph | telegraph | Ralph |
| photography | geography | Christopher |

## ph

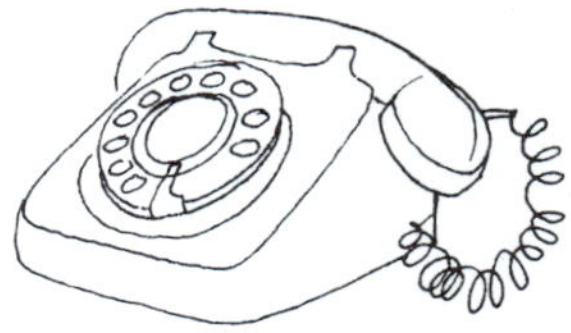

phone

## Exercise 1

## Exercise 2

Write down all the **ph** words you can see illustrated in this picture.

## Exercise 3

Write these sentences, filling in the missing words.

**1** We study ___________ and ______________ at school.
**2** A—Z is the ___________ .
**3** A ___________ is a bird.
**4** A child with no parents is an ___________ .

## pl

plant

| | |
|---|---|
| plant | plot |
| plank | plenty |
| plan | play |
| planet | plain |
| plug | plate |
| plum | plastic |
| plump | please |

### Exercise 1

### Exercise 2

Write down all the **pl** words you can see illustrated in this picture.

### Exercise 3

Write these sentences, filling in the missing words.

**1** Children like to _ _ _ _ games.
**2** We eat off a _ _ _ _ _ _ .
**3** A _ _ _ _ is a fruit.
**4** A flat piece of land is called a _ _ _ _ _ .
**5** We _ _ _ _ _ trees.

pram
prick
prickle
prize
press
present
proud

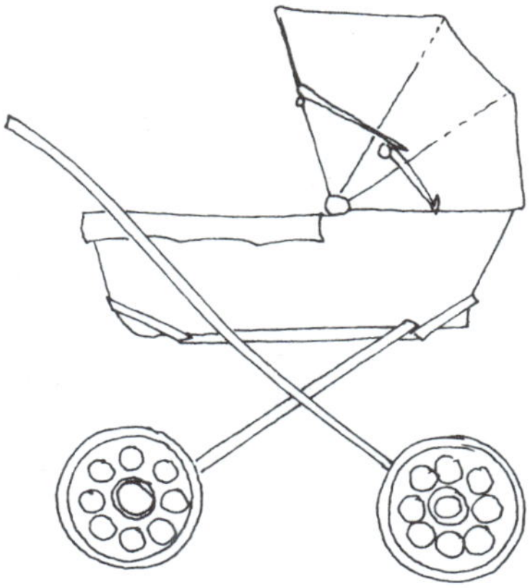

pram

pr

## Exercise 1

## Exercise 2

Draw and label these pictures.

Choose two more words to draw and label.

## Exercise 3

Write these sentences, filling in the missing words.

1 You may _ _ _ _ _ yourself on a thorn.
2 Mother gave me a _ _ _ _ _ _ _ for my birthday.
3 I won first _ _ _ _ _ in the race.
4 We can take baby out in a _ _ _ _ .
5 The teacher was _ _ _ _ _ of the clever children.

# ps

psalm

psalm
pseudo
psyche
psycho
psychic
psychology
psychologist
psychosis
psychotic
psychiatrist
psychiatry

## Exercise 1

## Exercise 2

This is a picture of a psychologist.

A psychiatrist's job is different. Either draw a psychiatrist at work or write a sentence describing it.

## Exercise 3

Write these sentences, filling in the missing words.

1 A _ _ _ _ _ _ _ _ _ _ _ _ _ is a doctor who treats mental illness.
2 Another word for soul is _ _ _ _ _ _ .
3 An educational _ _ _ _ _ _ _ _ _ _ _ _ _ helps people with learning difficulties.
4 We sing _ _ _ _ _s at church.

| | |
|---|---|
| scout | Scotland |
| scab | scrub |
| scamper | scream |
| scatter | scribble |
| scratch | |
| scramble | |
| scrape | |

scout

**sc**

## Exercise 1

## Exercise 2

Write down all the **sc** words you can see illustrated in this picture.

## Exercise 3

Write these sentences, filling in the missing words.

**1** _ _ _ _ _ _ _ _ _ is the country north of England.
**2** Mice _ _ _ _ _ _ _ _ .
**3** We _ _ _ _ _ with a brush.
**4** Finger nails can _ _ _ _ _ _ _ .
**5** We may _ _ _ _ _ _ _ the peel off new potatoes.

## sc

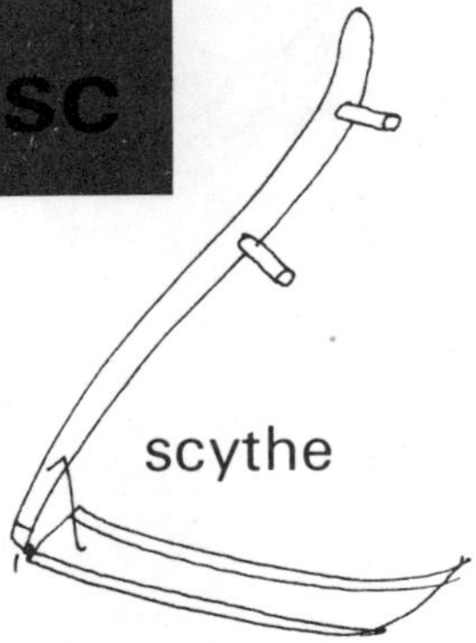


| | | |
|---|---|---|
| scythe | scent | conscience |
| scene | crescent | conscious |
| sceptre | scissors | unconscious |
| ascend | rescind | susceptible |
| ascent | muscle | scintillate |
| descend | ascertain | miscellaneous |
| descent | science | |

### Exercise 1

### Exercise 2

Draw and label these pictures.

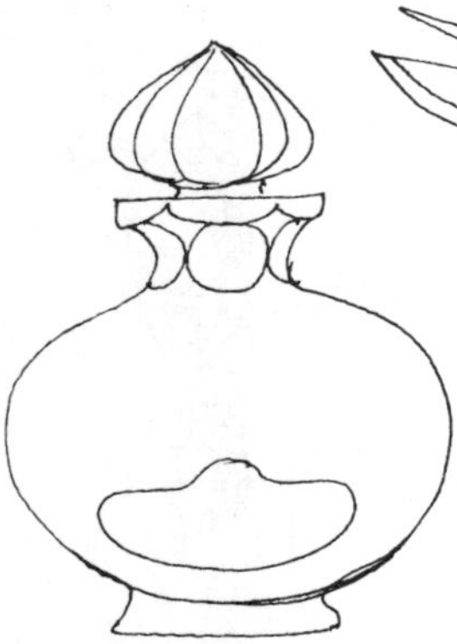

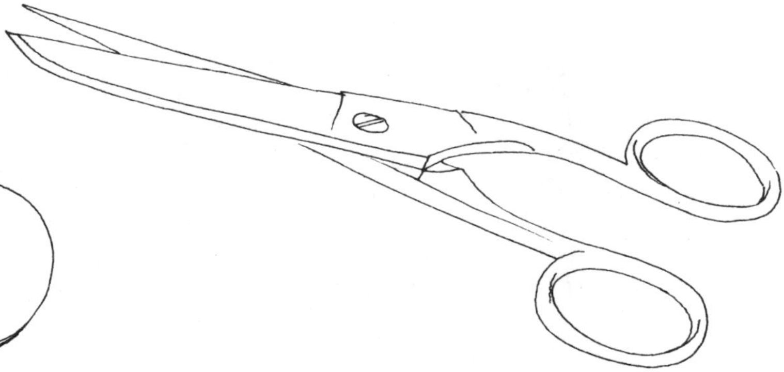

Choose two more words to draw and label.

### Exercise 3

Write these sentences, filling in the missing words.

1 We smell a _ _ _ _ _ .
2 To _ _ _ _ _ _ is to go up.
3 We cut cloth with a pair of _ _ _ _ _ _ _ _ .
4 A boxer who is knocked out is _ _ _ _ _ _ _ _ _ _ _ .
5 Our movements are controlled by our _ _ _ _ _ _s.

| | | |
|---|---|---|
| sheep | shake | wish |
| sheet | shape | dash |
| shed | shut | cash |
| shell | short | rush |
| should | shelter | hush |
| ship | dish | push |
| shop | fish | |

sheep

**sh**

## Exercise 1

## Exercise 2

Write down all the **sh** words you can see illustrated in this picture.

## Exercise 3

Write these sentences, filling in the missing words.

**1** To dash is to _ _ _ _ .
**2** A _ _ _ _ _ is a woolly animal.
**3** We buy things at a _ _ _ _ .
**4** A _ _ _ _ sails on the sea.
**5** Cod is a _ _ _ _ .

## sk

skate

skate
skin
skid
skip
skittle
sketch

### Exercise 1

### Exercise 2

Draw and label these pictures.

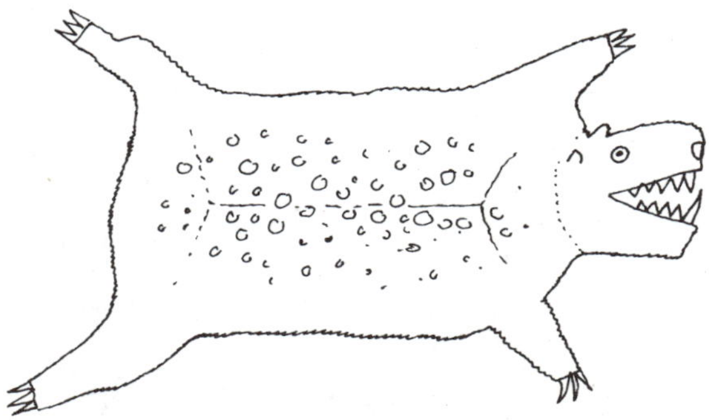

Choose two more words to draw and label.

### Exercise 3

Write these sentences, filling in the missing words.

1 The body is covered with ________ .
2 A car may ________ on ice.
3 We can ________ with a rope.
4 A rough drawing may be called a ________ .
5 There is a fish called ________ .

| | |
|---|---|
| slide | slot |
| slap | slim |
| slab | slip |
| slam | slipper |
| slack | slash |
| slant | slate |
| slope | sleep |

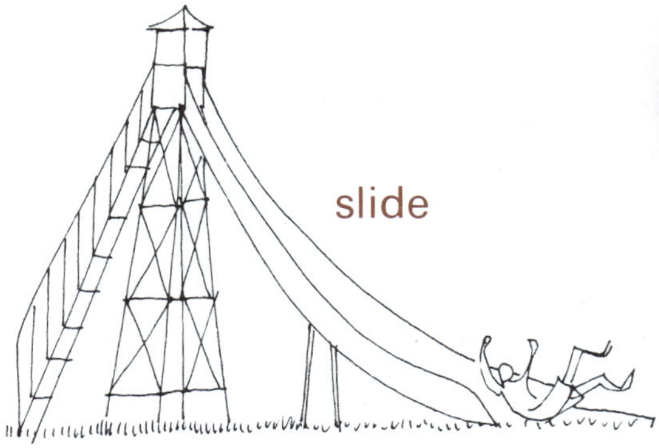


## sl

## Exercise 1

## Exercise 2

Draw and label these pictures.

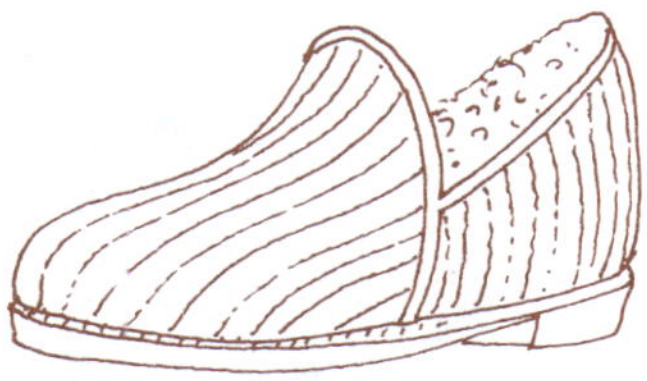

Choose two more words to draw and label.

## Exercise 3

Write these sentences, filling in the missing words.

**1** To hit is to _ _ _ _ .
**2** I go to _ _ _ _ _ _ at night.
**3** A thin person may be called _ _ _ _ .
**4** _ _ _ _ _ _ _s are worn on the feet.
**5** _ _ _ _ _ means loose.

# sm

smoke

smoke
smack
smash
smooth
small
smell
smile
smith
smart

## Exercise 1

## Exercise 2

Draw and label these pictures.

Choose two more words to draw and label.

## Exercise 3

Write these sentences, filling in the missing words.

**1** I can __ __ __ __ __ a nice perfume.
**2** __ __ __ __ __ __ is another word for even.
**3** Little means __ __ __ __ __ .
**4** __ __ __ __ __ comes from fire.
**5** A clever person is __ __ __ __ __ .

sn

snail
snake
snap
snatch
snow
snip
sniff
snug
sneeze

snail

## Exercise 1

## Exercise 2

Write down all the **sn** words you can see illustrated in this picture.

## Exercise 3

Write these sentences, filling in the missing words.

**1** To grab is to _ _ _ _ _ _ .
**2** An animal with its house on its back is called a _ _ _ _ _ .
**3** A _ _ _ _ _ is a reptile.
**4** _ _ _ _ is another word for cut.
**5** We ski on _ _ _ _ .

# sp

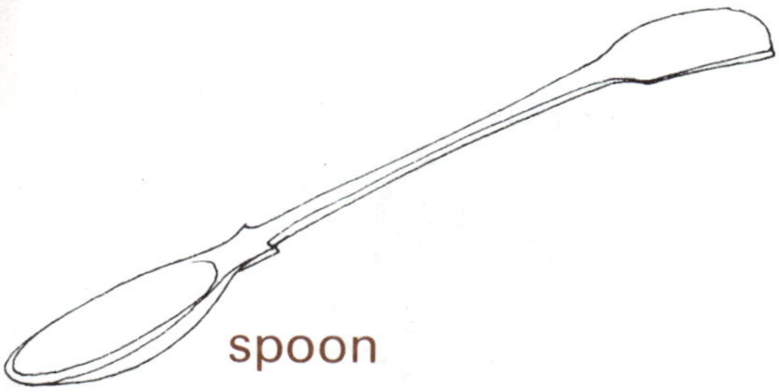


| | |
|---|---|
| spoon | speed |
| spit | splash |
| spin | spank |
| spill | spell |
| split | spend |
| spot | spent |

## Exercise 1

## Exercise 2

Write down all the **sp** words you can see illustrated in this picture.

## Exercise 3

Write these sentences, filling in the missing words.

1 To _ _ _ _ is to go round.
2 We stir things with a _ _ _ _ _ .
3 We _ _ _ _ _ money.
4 To _ _ _ _ _ is to go very fast.
5 We _ _ _ _ _ the word 'cat' with the letters c-a-t.

| | | | |
|---|---|---|---|
| stool | storm | post | east |
| stood | story | most | west |
| step | stone | ghost | rest |
| stick | stand | fast | test |
| still | start | last | must |
| stop | station | first | just |

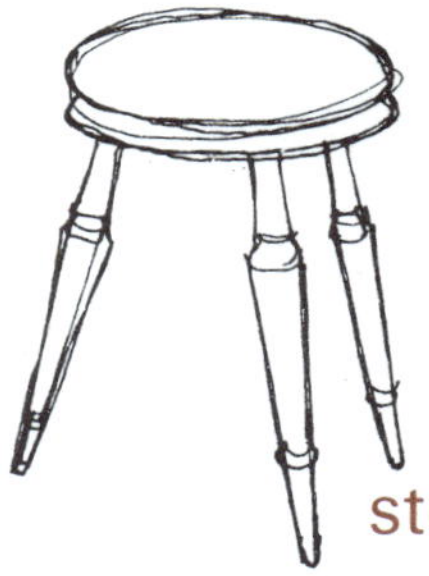

stool

**st**

## Exercise 1

## Exercise 2

Write down all the **st** words you can see illustrated in this picture.

## Exercise 3

Write these sentences, filling in the missing words.

**1** We catch a train at a _ _ _ _ _ _ _ .
**2** Teacher reads us a _ _ _ _ _ .
**3** A _ _ _ _ _ is a seat with three legs.
**4** We _ _ _ _ _ on our feet.
**5** We _ _ _ _ letters in a pillar box.

# sw

sweep

sweep
sweet
swell
sway
swing
swim
switch

## Exercise 1

## Exercise 2

Draw and label these pictures.

Choose two more words to draw and label.

## Exercise 3

Write these sentences, filling in the missing words.

1 Sugar is __ __ __ __ __ .
2 We __ __ __ __ __ __ on a light.
3 We __ __ __ __ __ with a brush.
4 A __ __ __ __ __ goes backwards and forwards.
5 We can __ __ __ __ in the sea or at the baths.

| | | |
|---|---|---|
| thimble | thaw | month |
| three | theatre | path |
| third | theory | bath |
| thirteen | thick | north |
| thank | thigh | south |
| thin | thirst | mouth |
| theft | thistle | tenth |
| think | moth | tooth |
| throne | cloth | teeth |

| | |
|---|---|
| the | them |
| they | with |
| their | without |
| this | father |
| that | mother |
| than | brother |
| there | other |
| these | another |
| those | gather |
| then | clothes |

**th**

thimble

## Exercise 1

## Exercise 2

Write down all the **th** words you can see illustrated in this picture.

## Exercise 3

Write these sentences, filling in the missing words.

**1** My mother's son is my ____________ .
**2** Six is one more ________ five.
**3** A ________ is an insect.
**4** __________ and __________ are directions.

# tr

tree

| | | |
|---|---|---|
| tree | train | travel |
| treat | trade | tractor |
| try | track | truck |
| trick | trap | trunk |
| trip | traffic | trust |
| trouble | tramp | trumpet |
| troop | | |

## Exercise 1

## Exercise 2

Write down all the **tr** words you can see illustrated in this picture.

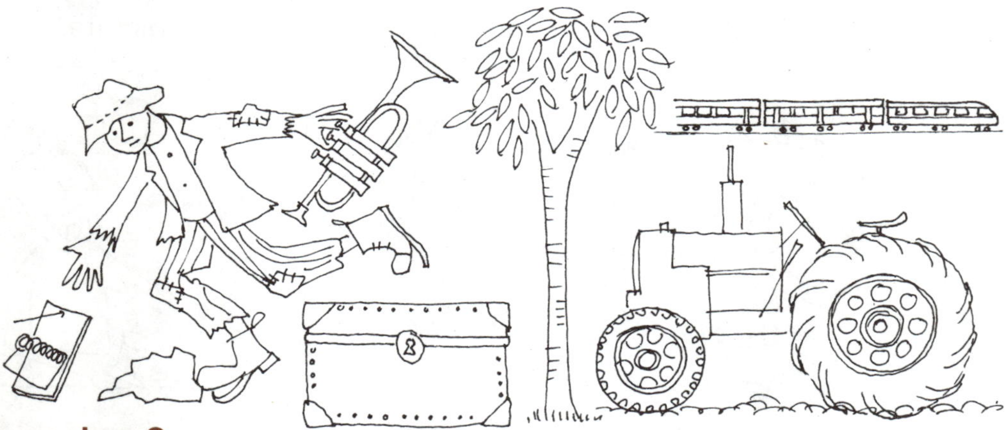

## Exercise 3

Write these sentences, filling in the missing words.

**1** A _ _ _ _ _ runs on rails.
**2** Americans call a lorry a _ _ _ _ _ .
**3** A _ _ _ _ _ has no home.
**4** A _ _ _ _ _ _ _ is a musical instrument.
**5** A _ _ _ _ has branches.

twig
twin
twist
twinkle
twenty
twelve

twig

# tw

## Exercise 1

## Exercise 2

Draw and label these pictures.

Choose two more words to draw and label.

## Exercise 3

Write these sentences, filling in the missing words.

1 A dozen is __ __ __ __ __ __ .
2 __ __ __ __ __ __ comes after nineteen.
3 Two children born at the same time are called __ __ __ __s.
4 A __ __ __ __ is found on a branch.
5 A star __ __ __ __ __ __ __s.

# wh

wheel

| | | |
|---|---|---|
| wheel | why | whisper |
| wheat | which | what |
| when | whip | |
| whether | whisk | |
| while | whisker | |
| white | whistle | |
| where | whimper | whole |

## Exercise 1

## Exercise 2

Write down all the **wh** words you can see illustrated in this picture.

## Exercise 3

Write these sentences, filling in the missing words.

**1** To speak softly is to _ _ _ _ _ _ _ .
**2** "_ _ _ _ _ are you going?" asked mother.
**3** "_ _ _ _ do you want?" asked the teacher.
**4** "_ _ _ _ did you arrive?" asked my friend.
**5** "_ _ _ did you do that?" asked father.

# wr

wreath
wreck
wreckage
wren
wrench
wretch
write
writing
written
wrote
wring
wrinkle
wriggle
wrist
wrong

wreath

## Exercise 1

## Exercise 2

Write down all the **wr** words you can see illustrated in this picture.

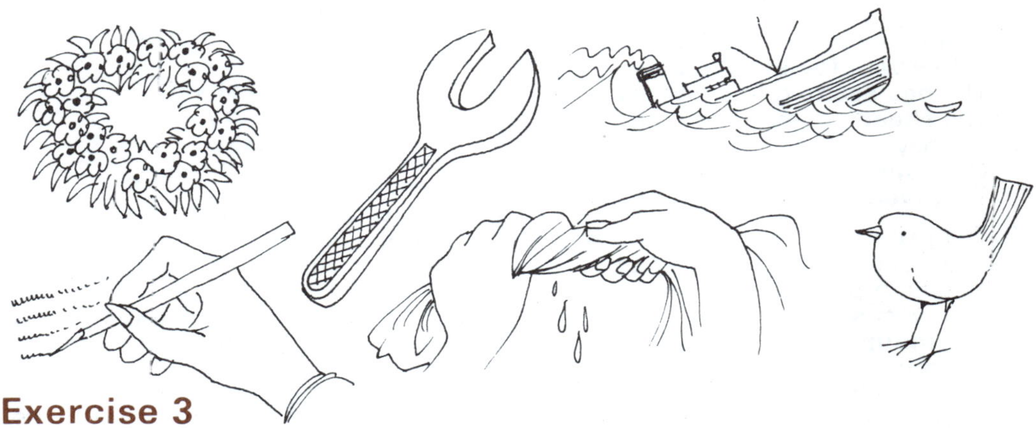

## Exercise 3

Write these sentences, filling in the missing words.

**1** My _ _ _ _ _ is between my arm and my hand.
**2** A _ _ _ _ is a bird.
**3** We should _ _ _ _ _ a letter in our best hand_ _ _ _ _ _ _ .
**4** It is _ _ _ _ _ to be bad.

# Tests

4 Bill was **hitting**,
Jill was **sitting**,
Dad was **batting**,
Mum was **patting**.

5 Bob **missed** the ball. Bill **dashed** after it. Bob **rushed** at Bill and **pushed** him. Bill **picked** up the ball and **passed** it to Tim.

6 The **killer** was **madder** and **sadder** than **ever**, as the **winner** was a **bigger** and **better swimmer** than him.

7 Bob was the **fattest** and **dullest** boy in the club but he was the **fastest** runner. He ran **faster** than the **thinnest** and **fittest** boys and his mother and father said he was the best.

8 **Daddy** and **mummy** were **very happy** with the **puppy** in the **lorry**. It was **sunny** and **windy** and they had to **hurry** up the **hilly** land.

9 A **sheep** went to **meet** a **bee**
A **bee** with **feelers** you **see**
The **bee seemed** to be **needy**
The **sheep seemed** very **seedy**
So they were **greedy**
On **sweet peel** and **cheese**
That **week** of the **deepest freeze**.

10 The **proud scout** showed that he was not silly and that he could catch a **mouse**. He left the **house** and went **south**. **Round** the hill, **out** of a **mound** in the **ground**, **pounced** a **mouse**. With a **loud shout**, the **scout** grabbed the **mouse**, **wound** it up in rags and **bounded** home.

11 In the **east** the **heat** is **wearying** so men sip **tea** and **speak peacefully**. But in England the **seasons** are **easy** and we **dream** of **leaves**, **wheat**, **peaceful streams** and the **dear sea**.

12 The **farmer parked** his **car**
Too near the **yard** by **far**.
In the **dark**
He saw a **spark**
That put a **mark**
Upon his **car**—a fire in the **barn**.

13 On **Sunday** we **pray**,
On **Monday** we **say**
"**Tuesday** is **hay day**."
On **Wednesday** we **pay**,
On **Thursday** we **say**
"**Friday** is **pay day**."
But on **Saturday** we are **gay**
For on **Saturday** we **play**.
**Always** gone is **yesterday**
**Always** with us is **today**.

14 I went to **Spain**
But left my **brain**
On the **train**.
So I got a **chain**
To get it back **again**.
It must be **plain**
I need my **brain**.

15 The **goat** on the **road** saw the **coal boat floating** fully **loaded** on the **broad** river.

16 "Oh **my**" said the **fly**
As he went up in the **sky**
"I want to be **by myself**."
But a bee went **by**
So the **fly** was **shy**
And started to **cry**
Up in the **dry sky**.

17 **Late** at the **gate**
He **gave** a **wave**
To the man with a **name**
Which was just the **same**.

18 **White mice** are **quite nice** but a **wife** with a **knife** and a **nice smile** is better.

19 The **gnome rode home alone** as the **mole dozed** in his **hole**.

20 In **June** the **duke** on a **mule** sang a **rude tune** to **amuse** and **cure** his **pure mule**.

21 The **ball** was **falling** in the **hall**. A **tall** lad and a **small** one ran for it. Jim **called** out: "Stop or you will hit the **wall**." **All** the lads, from the **tallest** to the **smallest**, **called** "Stop!" The **smallest** lad got the **ball**.

22 In the **light** was a **frightful sight**
Two **mighty** men were **tight** in a **fight**
Were they **right** to have a **fight**
On such a **bright light night**?
The moon was **high**
They did not **sigh**
But one took **fright**
And dashed off on a **flight**.

23 **How now brown cow**
Who **drowned** the **sow**?
"She just went **down**
She did not **drown**"
Said the **frowning, howling clown**.
"She was **showered** with **flowers**"
Said the **owl** to the **fowl**.

24 The man with a **fiddle**
Had a **pimple** on his **middle**
But it was only **little**
And he was only **simple**
So he got a **candle**
And set fire to his **fiddle**.

25 **Soon** it will be **noon**
Gone will be the **moon**
Back from **school**
Will run a **fool**
With a **broom** for a **tool**.
He will pick a **root**
He will give a **hoot**
He will kick his **boot**
Into the **pool**.
He is no **good**
He picks no **wood**
He plays in **soot**
He will not **look**
The **foolish goofy fool**!

26 The **horse** had a **fork** stuck in his leg. As he could not **afford** a **doctor**, he asked **Porky** to take it out for him. A **north storm shortly formed** so **Porky** took a **torch** and quickly extracted the **fork** from the **torn** leg.

27 Do you **know** a plant that **grows**?
Do you **know** a river that **flows**?
Do you **know** a wind that **blows**?
Have you seen any **yellow crows**?
I **know** a **fellow**
Who went **slowly yellow**
For **throwing** an **arrow**
At a **slowly** flying **sparrow**.

28 Jim wanted to **capture** a **creature** with a **fracture**. He had seen an **adventure picture** in a **scripture** book where a man had used a **mixture** of seeds and had **captured** such a **creature**. Jim found a **vulture** but could not **capture** it.

29 **Ready steady** go
We're off to a **pleasant** show
We feel very **healthy**
We feel very **wealthy**
Look at the **weather**
Look at the **heather**
**Ready steady** go.

30 The **girl** put on her **shirt** and **skirt**. She was **thirteen** and having a **birthday** party. She gave the food a **stir**, moved the **bird** up higher and made its cage **firm**. She was then ready for the **first girl** to come.

31 The **wasp** on the **washing was watching** the **swan swallow water** in the **swamp**.

32 The **squadron** in **quarantine quarrelled** about the **quantity** and **quality** of the orange **squash**.

33 Up the **staircase** ran **Claire**
Once more she swung her **hair**
She jumped over a **chair**
Fell down in **despair**
And could not be **repaired**.

34 "My **word**, it is true," said the **worm** to the **world's worst worker**. "Your **work** is not **worth** a **word**." "I **work** with his **worship** Mr. **Wormwood**," said the **world's worst worker**, "and my **work** is **worth** more than a **worm's**."

35 They **bought nought**
They **brought nought**
They **sought nought**
They **thought nought** worth doing
They only **fought** and **fought**.

36 The **mare stared** at the word **BEWARE**. She had been **dared** to go past it, but she was **scared** for her **welfare**. If I do not take **care**, she thought, I may not be **spared**, so I will **BEWARE**.

37 My **nephew** was a **Jew**
And always liked to **chew**
He **chewed** his **stew**
And **grew** a **yew**
And never **knew**
There were so **few**
Who could **screw** a **screw**.

38 On **Thursday** Mrs. **Turner** got a nasty **burn** when she was filling the tea **urn**. It **hurt** very much so she **turned** to a **nurse** for help. The **nurse** took an old **curtain** and wound it round the **burn**. She told Mrs. **Turner** to **return** on **Saturday** for **further nursing**.

39 The **earl** was out **early searching** for **pearls**. He had **heard** that there were many in the **earth**. When he did not find any in the **earth** he asked **earnestly**: "Which part of the **earth** has **pearls**?" He soon **learned** to **search** the sea, not the **earth**, for **pearls**.

40 The **jackdaw** with a **raw claw**
Put his **paw** in his **jaw**
Until he **saw dawn**
**Draw** over the **lawn**.

41 A **boy** called **Roy**
Found **joy** in his **toy**.
"Do not **destroy** it
He wants to **enjoy** it."
Called out a **royal** voice.

42 Can you **join** a **coin** with a **coil** of **foil**?
Can you **spoil** the **soil** with a squirt of **oil**?
Can you make a **noise** in your softest **voice**?
Or **boil** a **boiler**?
Or **point** a **pointer**?

43 The **thief** ran off the **pier** and into a **field**, chased by the **chief** of police who **believed** that the **thief** would soon need a **brief** rest. He did, so the police **chief** caught him. The **chief** judge **reprieved** the **thief** on condition that he saw his **niece** and the **priest**. The family were very **relieved**.

44 The **conceited** man stuck the **receipt** on the **ceiling**.

45 **Neither** the boy by the **weir** nor the man who **seized** the dog saw the **weird** monster.

46 "My **son** has **done** a **ton** of **honey**
We should **come** into a lot of **money**"
Said a **London mother** to her **other brother**.
"Last **month** it was a **dozen comfortable gloves**
The **month** before he **won some monkeys**."

47 **Before** you **snore** any **more**
Do not **bore** us with the **score**
Bring **ashore** an apple **core**
From the **store** that I **adore**.

48 A **monkey**, a **turkey** and a **donkey** climbed a **chimney**. They wanted **honey**, **money** and a **key** but as they had failed they went to play **hockey** in the **valley**.

49 In a country **borough**
There lived Mr. **Thorough**.
He was **rough** and **tough enough**
Though he fell in a **trough**
And started to **cough**
And pushed the **plough**
Into a **bough**.

50 The **audience applauded automatically** as the **author** took his bow. In the play the **automatic saucer** had fallen on the **tarpaulin** roof of a **laundry** and **caused** a **fault** in the **automatic** machines. Because the play had been so awful **Paul** and **Audrey** walked out.

51 The **young couple** went to the **country** to visit their **cousin**. They ate four **double** beefburgers for **nourishment**. When rain **troubled** them they ran fourteen miles back home.

52 **Eight** tons of **freight** is a very great **weight** to throw on a **neighbour's sleigh** from a **height**.

53 The **dwarf** with a **wart warmed** his hands by the **warming** fire. He leaned **forward** only to be **rewarded** with the **warning** that the **warmth** would burn off his **wart**.

54 The **quartet** played a **quarter** of the tune, wearing **quartz** watches.

55 **Mary's parent** was a **librarian caring** for the **library area**.

56 When I **mentioned** the **direction** of the **station** he jumped to **attention** and sprang into **action**.

57 The **door** and **floor** of the **poor** house on the **moor** were rotten.

58 **Tie** a knot in your **tie**
**Lie** down when you **die**
But don't spoil the **pie**.

59 Is it **true** that **glue** is **blue**?

60 The **doe's foe** put the **hoe** through his **shoe** and his **toe**.

61 Can you **wound** a **group** with a **soup coupon**?

62 Be **resourceful** and **pour yourself four** glasses of water.

63 As the **fruit** was **bruised** the people on the **cruise** said it was not **suitable fruit** to eat so they drank **fruit juice** instead.

64 Tip your **oar**
Do not **roar**.
The bird will **soar**
**Overboard**,
Its voice is **hoarse**
And very **coarse**.

65 **Half** a **calm calf** sat in a **palm** tree eating **almonds** and singing a **psalm**.

66 People sometimes **walk**
A flower has a **stalk**
Our teacher uses **chalk**
And sometimes lets us **talk**.

67 He **caught** his **naughty daughter**
And **taught** her how to **slaughter**
At which there was much **laughter**.

68 You should not shrug your **shoulders**
You should not break up **boulders**
If your temper **smoulders**
You should pray to save your **soul**.

69 Are you **sure** there is the **usual measure** of **sugar** to give **pleasure** to those who **treasure** their syrup?

70 **My cycle** has a **nylon tyre** of the **type styled** for long wear.

71 The **mysterious physical symptom** in his **lymph** was **systematically** and **sympathetically syringed**.

72 The **quick squirrel quivered** and **squeaked** when the **quiet queen squirted liquid** at him.

73 **Listen** to my **solemn** tale
Of a **tongue** lost in a gale
Caught in a **pneumatic** drill
Last **autumn** near a **sword's** hilt.

# Answers

| Page | | |
|---|---|---|
| 4 | **Ex 2** boxing shopping sitting patting winning batting singing | **Ex 3 1** singing **2** patting **3** shopping **4** sitting **5** batting |
| 5 | **Ex 2** tinned tripped pushed slipped kissed hopped | **Ex 3 1** filled **2** padded **3** hopped **4** passed **5** tripped |
| 6 | **Ex 2** killer number dinner father mother person finger winter runner | **Ex 3 1** dinner (supper) **2** summer **3** fingers **4** number **5** killer |
| 7 | **Ex 2** fattest biggest oddest fullest hottest | **Ex 3 1** fastest **2** biggest **3** oddest **4** hottest **5** fullest |
| 8 | **Ex 2** holly hilly puppy mummy daddy windy lorry jelly | **Ex 3 1** lorry **2** daddy **3** silly, holly **4** funny |
| 9 | **Ex 2** sweet cheese freeze feet peel sheep bee feeler | **Ex 3 1** sheep **2** bee **3** street **4** cheese **5** feel |
| 10 | **Ex 2** fountain house cloud mountain trousers pound scout trout | **Ex 3 1** trout **2** mouse **3** sour **4** mountain **5** round |
| 11 | **Ex 2** heat sea seat read leap reach ear eat tea beach | **Ex 3 1** seal **2** seat **3** hear, ear **4** season |
| 12 | **Ex 2** farmer scarf arm car star parking marching barking | **Ex 3 1** car **2** farm **3** ark **4** start **5** are |
| 13 | **Ex 2** day ray hay play lay pay | **Ex 3 1** days **2** play **3** Friday **4** pray **5** clay |
| 14 | **Ex 2** waiter rain painter railing railway waiting sailor | **Ex 3 1** train **2** rains **3** nail **4** painted **5** sail |
| 15 | **Ex 2** loaf toast toaster coal coat cloak goal soaked | **Ex 3 1** oak **2** goat, foal (toad) **3** road **4** oats **5** goal |
| 16 | **Ex 2** shy sty fly cry fry spy | **Ex 3 1** fly **2** sky **3** fry **4** sly **5** multiply |
| 17 | **Ex 2** cake cage wave race game gate late | **Ex 3 1** cake **2** game **3** name **4** race **5** safe, safe |
| 18 | **Ex 2** ice fire nine mile five mice bike wife knife smile | **Ex 3 1** bike **2** nine **3** five **4** knife **5** mice |
| 19 | **Ex 2** nose rose smoke home bone rope gnome pole stone | **Ex 3 1** alone **2** smokes **3** stone **4** mole **5** spokes |
| 20 | **Ex 2** rude cube duke mule tube | **Ex 3 1** cube **2** mule **3** amuses **4** tune **5** use |
| 21 | **Ex 2** tallest ball wall falling smallest | **Ex 3 1** ball **2** fall **3** smaller **4** stall **5** all |
| 22 | **Ex 2** knight fright night flight fight | **Ex 3 1** night, light **2** flight **3** frightened **4** lighter |
| 23 | **Ex 2** owl crown fowl sow clown trowel flower shower crowd | **Ex 3 1** cow (sow) **2** owl **3** allow **4** towel **5** trowel |
| 24 | **Ex 2** saddle bundle apple fiddle bangle candle bottle table | **Ex 3 1** bottle **2** table **3** candle **4** fiddle **5** apple |
| 25 | **Ex 2** fool book boot balloon moon wood hoop zoo tool broom food | **Ex 3 1** fool **2** good **3** books, school **4** looked |
| 26 | **Ex 2** corn horse storm fort doctor torch stork | **Ex 3 1** storm **2** story **3** sport **4** pork **5** doctor |
| 27 | **Ex 2** grower bowl bow snow barrow elbow crow arrow | **Ex 3 1** know, blows **2** bow, arrow **3** yellow |
| 28 | **Ex 2** pasture puncture signature capture creature torture | **Ex 3 1** fracture **2** furniture **3** puncture **4** vulture **5** pasture |
| 29 | **Ex 2** bread breakfast treasure measure dead weapon feather healthy heavy | **Ex 3 1** breakfast **2** thread **3** read **4** weather **5** heavy |
| 30 | **Ex 2** thirsty dirt skirt shirt stirring girl birthday thirteen | **Ex 3 1** thirsty **2** stirred **3** birthday **4** thirteen **5** girl, dirty |

**31** **Ex 2** wallet swan watch wand wash
**Ex 3** **1** wasp **2** washing **3** swan **4** watch **5** swallow

**32** **Ex 2** squash quarantine quarrel
**Ex 3** **1** quarantine **2** squash **3** squadron **4** quarrel **5** squat

**33** **Ex 2** stair fairy repair chair hairy pair
**Ex 3** **1** pair **2** dairy **3** hair **4** repair **5** chair

**34** **Ex 2** worm work
**Ex 3** **1** worker **2** worship **3** word **4** worm **5** world

**35** **Ex 2** thought fought
**Ex 3** **1** bought **2** thought **3** nought **4** fought **5** brought

**36** **Ex 2** careless BEWARE square hare mare
**Ex 3** **1** hare (mare) **2** BEWARE **3** spare **4** square **5** fare

**37** **Ex 2** jewel newspaper screw yew ewe threw stew
**Ex 3** **1** flew **2** chew **3** crew **4** knew **5** yew

**38** **Ex 2** purse church nurse hamburger curly curtain murder turnip turkey
**Ex 3** **1** turnip **2** turkey **3** hurt **4** curtain **5** Saturn

**39** **Ex 2** learner hearse searching pearl
**Ex 3** **1** learn **2** pearl **3** early **4** hearse **5** earth

**40** **Ex 2** yawn jaw shawl drawer dawn paw
**Ex 3** **1** hawk, jackdaw **2** paw **3** claw **4** yawn **5** dawn

**41** **Ex 2** annoyed destroyed boy Roy enjoy toy convoy buoy destroyer
**Ex 3** **1** toy **2** boy **3** Roy **4** enjoy **5** voyage

**42** **Ex 2** choir coin boil coil noisy pointing joiner
**Ex 3** **1** coin **2** soil **3** boil **4** ointment **5** joiner

**43** **Ex 2** shield chief priest niece thief pier field
**Ex 3** **1** grieve **2** field **3** thief **4** niece **5** chief

**44** **Ex 2** receipt receiving
**Ex 3** **1** ceiling **2** receipt **3** conceited **4** perceive **5** deceive

**45** **Ex 2** weir weird
**Ex 3** **1** weird **2** seize **3** weir **4** neither **5** either

**46** **Ex 2** honey shovel mother monkey sponge glove
**Ex 3** **1** London **2** months **3** worry **4** honey **5** son

**47** **Ex 2** snore core swore sore adore tore
**Ex 3** **1** core **2** shore **3** score **4** before **5** more

**48** **Ex 2** chimney valley donkey hockey monkey key money
**Ex 3** **1** donkey **2** chimney **3** key **4** money **5** monkey, donkey

**49** **Ex 2** trough dough bough cough
**Ex 3** **1** tough **2** thorough **3** ploughed **4** cough **5** although

**50** **Ex 2** automatic laundry (Santa) Claus saucer astronaut vault applaud
**Ex 3** **1** author **2** saucer **3** Claus **4** Paul, Pauline

**51** **Ex 2** country young couple touching nourishment trouble
**Ex 3** **1** touch **2** trouble **3** nourishment **4** country **5** cousin

**52** **Ex 2** reindeer rein sleigh eight neighbour
**Ex 3** **1** neighbours **2** neighs **3** veins **4** eighty **5** their

**53** **Ex 2** war ward dwarf wart
**Ex 3** **1** swarm **2** ward **3** warm **4** reward **5** war

**54** **Ex 2** quarter quartz
**Ex 3** **1** quarter **2** quartet **3** quartz **4** quart

**55** **Ex 2** scaring library
**Ex 3** **1** library **2** scarce **3** Mary **4** canary **5** parents

**56** **Ex 2** position reflection station destination collection
**Ex 3** **1** reflection **2** destination **3** nation **4** station **5** direction

**57** **Ex 2** door floor
**Ex 3** **1** floor **2** poor **3** moor **4** door

**58** **Ex 2** tie pie
**Ex 3** **1** pie **2** die **3** tie **4** lie

**59** **Ex 2** glue clue
**Ex 3** **1** blue **2** glue **3** value **4** true **5** clue

**60** **Ex 2** hoe doe
**Ex 3** **1** hoe **2** foe **3** doe **4** toes **5** shoe

**61** **Ex 2** soup group
**Ex 3** **1** coupon **2** soup **3** group **4** you **5** wound

**62** **Ex 2** four pour
**Ex 3** **1** fourteen **2** your **3** four **4** pour **5** favourite

| | | |
|---|---|---|
| **63** | **Ex 2** cruise suit fruit juice | **Ex 3 1** fruit **2** cruise **3** suit **4** juice **5** bruise |
| **64** | **Ex 2** overboard oar roar boar | **Ex 3 1** oars **2** cupboard **3** roars **4** boar **5** soared |
| **65** | **Ex 2** calf calm almonds palm | **Ex 3 1** calf **2** half **3** calm **4** almonds **5** palm |
| **66** | **Ex 2** walk talk | **Ex 3 1** walk **2** talk **3** chalk **4** stalk |
| **67** | **Ex 2** laugh naughty daughter caught slaughter | **Ex 3 1** taught **2** caught **3** slaughter **4** daughter **5** naughty |
| **68** | **Ex 2** shoulder boulder | **Ex 3 1** boulder **2** shoulder **3** souls **4** smoulder **5** mouldy |
| **69** | **Ex 2** measure treasure | **Ex 3 1** sugar **2** measure **3** pleasure **4** sure **5** usually |
| **70** | **Ex 2** typewriter python pylon xylophone cycle hyacinth | **Ex 3 1** cycle **2** python **3** byre **4** dynamite **5** cyclone (typhoon) |
| **71** | **Ex 2** pyramid symmetry gym sycamore cymbal | **Ex 3 1** syrup **2** hymns **3** sycamore **4** physics **5** mystery |
| **72** | **Ex 2** queen squeeze squirt liquid squirrel quill quilt | **Ex 3 1** liquid **2** quack **3** quiet **4** quench **5** quick |
| **73** | **Ex 2** pneumatic listen sword racquet bouquet | **Ex 3 1** racquet **2** pneumatic **3** autumn **4** listen **5** sword |
| **74** | **Ex 2** plumber tomb bomb comb lamb crumb | **Ex 3 1** comb **2** lamb **3** plumber **4** thumb **5** debt |
| **75** | **Ex 2** blacksmith blanket blazer bleed blood blade blind black | **Ex 3 1** blanket **2** bleat **3** blind **4** bleed **5** black |
| **76** | **Ex 2** brave bride brow brush brandy broom broken | **Ex 3 1** brown **2** broke **3** brandy **4** bricks **5** brook |
| **77** | **Ex 2** cheap cheese child choose cheek chin check cherry chestnut church chest | **Ex 3 1** cherry **2** cheap **3** child **4** cheese **5** chain |
| **78** | **Ex 2** chorus chrysanthemum scholar mechanic chaos | **Ex 3 1** Christmas **2** headache **3** orchestra **4** cholera **5** echo |
| **79** | **Ex 2** truck sack back cock duck neck packet kick Jack sock stick rock chicken | **Ex 3 1** kick **2** duck **3** Dick, Jack **4** lick (suck) |
| **80** | **Ex 2** clutch club cliff cling cloud | **Ex 3 1** clap **2** clumsy **3** clock **4** clouds **5** clever |
| **81** | **Ex 2** crash crab cream crutch crooked cross crumb | **Ex 3 1** crimson **2** crab **3** crust **4** crooked **5** cross |
| **82** | **Ex 2** dress drink drip drop dragon driver drum | **Ex 3 1** dragon **2** draw **3** dress **4** drank **5** drive (drove) |
| **83** | **Ex 2** cuff sniff toffee coffee | **Ex 3 1** toffee **2** coffee **3** stiff **4** off **5** sniff |
| **84** | **Ex 2** flock flower flutter flag flask fleet | **Ex 3 1** fly **2** flour **3** flock **4** flower **5** flames |
| **85** | **Ex 2** frock frog frame frost | **Ex 3 1** free **2** frock **3** frog **4** freezes **5** frame |
| **86** | **Ex 2** glass glue globe glove | **Ex 3 1** glider **2** glad **3** glossy **4** glass **5** glue |
| **87** | **Ex 2** gnarled gnu | **Ex 3 1** sign **2** gnome **3** gnaws **4** gnat **5** reigns |
| **88** | **Ex 2** grapes grin grab greedy grand grave growl ground gravel grass | **Ex 3 1** ground, grave **2** green **3** grapes **4** grab |
| **89** | **Ex 2** dinghy rhinoceros | **Ex 3 1** rhubarb **2** dinghy **3** rhinoceros **4** honest **5** John |
| **90** | **Ex 2** knot knife knight knob knee kneel knuckle | **Ex 3 1** knew **2** knee **3** knife **4** knuckle **5** knot |
| **91** | **Ex 2** camp hamper empty imp tramp lamp limp hump jumper shampoo | **Ex 3 1** shampoo **2** pump **3** limp **4** lamp **5** jumper |
| **92** | **Ex 2** wind hand stand band pond | **Ex 3 1** stand **2** spend **3** hand **4** band **5** wind |
| **93** | **Ex 2** tank sprinkle link bunk wink ankle ink | **Ex 3 1** pink **2** wink **3** bunk **4** spank **5** sink |
| **94** | **Ex 2** hunt print lantern winter tent | **Ex 3 1** sent **2** spent **3** ant **4** tent **5** winter |

**95** **Ex 2** graph alphabet pheasant photograph phone elephant
**Ex 3** **1** physics, geography **2** alphabet **3** pheasant **4** orphan

**96** **Ex 2** play plump plug plant plan plum plate
**Ex 3** **1** play **2** plate **3** plum **4** plain **5** plant

**97** **Ex 2** present prick
**Ex 3** **1** prick **2** present **3** prize **4** pram **5** proud

**98** **Ex 2** psychologist
**Ex 3** **1** psychiatrist **2** psyche **3** psychologist **4** psalms

**99** **Ex 2** scout scrub scrape scatter Scotland
**Ex 3** **1** Scotland **2** scamper **3** scrub **4** scratch **5** scrape

**100** **Ex 2** scent scissors
**Ex 3** **1** scent **2** ascend **3** scissors **4** unconscious **5** muscles

**101** **Ex 2** ship shelter shed shell fish dish sheet sheep
**Ex 3** **1** rush **2** sheep **3** shop **4** ship **5** fish

**102** **Ex 2** skip skin
**Ex 3** **1** skin **2** skid **3** skip **4** sketch **5** skate

**103** **Ex 2** slipper sleep
**Ex 3** **1** slap **2** sleep **3** slim **4** slippers **5** slack

**104** **Ex 2** smile smack
**Ex 3** **1** smell **2** smooth **3** small **4** smoke **5** smart

**105** **Ex 2** snake snail snow sniff sneeze snug
**Ex 3** **1** snatch **2** snail **3** snake **4** snip **5** snow

**106** **Ex 2** spin spill splash spot spent
**Ex 3** **1** spin **2** spoon **3** spend **4** speed **5** spell

**107** **Ex 2** post ghost stool stick east west
**Ex 3** **1** station **2** story **3** stool **4** stand **5** post

**108** **Ex 2** swim sweep
**Ex 3** **1** sweet **2** switch **3** sweep **4** swing **5** swim

**109** **Ex 2** thimble three theft cloth clothes moth thistle mouth teeth thirst
**Ex 3** **1** brother **2** than **3** moth **4** north, south

**110** **Ex 2** trap trip tramp trumpet trunk tree train tractor
**Ex 3** **1** train **2** truck **3** tramp **4** trumpet **5** tree

**111** **Ex 2** twelve twig
**Ex 3** **1** twelve **2** twenty **3** twins **4** twig **5** twinkles

**112** **Ex 2** whisker whip wheel whistle whisper wheat
**Ex 3** **1** whisper **2** where **3** what **4** when **5** why

**113** **Ex 2** wreath write writing wrist wrench wring wreck wren
**Ex 3** **1** wrist **2** wren **3** write, handwriting **4** wrong

# Part III—common words for reference

The following common words are either irregular or are needed for both reading and writing in advance of learning their relevant spelling pattern. Each student should compile an alphabetical list of them for reference. He may consult a word when necessary but must **not** copy it. He should study it then write it from memory (see notes for teachers 6, page 127).

**One hundred common words**

answer
any
beauty
bicycle
biscuit
break
Britain
bruise
build
bury
busy
buy
cafe
calm
castle
Christmas
colonel
cough
country
cousin
daughter
do
does
double
dozen
Dr.
England
enough
ever
every
eye
four
friend
fruit
grandparents
great
grey
half
heart
height
honest
hour
iron
island
journey
language
laugh
listen
lose
machine
many
minute
move
Mr.
Mrs.
neighbour
nephew
niece
obey
often
once
one
parents
people
police
pretty
prove
question
said
says
school
scissors
sew
shoe
shoulder
sign
son
steak
sugar
suit
sure
sword
talk
that
they
to
tongue
uncle
usual
very
walk
water
what
whistle
who
whole
women
you
young
your

**Numbers**

nought quarter half one two three four five six seven eight nine
ten eleven twelve thirteen fifteen twenty thirty forty fifty hundred
thousand million
first second third fourth fifth twelfth twentieth twenty-first hundredth

**Months of the year**

January February March April May June July August September
October November December

**Days of the week**

Sunday Monday Tuesday Wednesday Thursday Friday Saturday

**Seasons**
spring summer autumn winter

**Colours**
black blue brown green grey lilac navy orange pink purple red scarlet turquoise white yellow

**The classroom**
carpet ceiling chair cupboard curtain desk door (knob) easel floor notice-board shelf sink tap window

# Part IV— practice words

Students who have difficulty with syllabication can practise with the following words. The words should each be written on a separate card with a space between the syllables. e.g. blan ket
spoil ing

The student looks at and says the word in the usual way until he thinks he knows it.

**Two-syllable words—short vowel**

| | | | | | | | |
|---|---|---|---|---|---|---|---|
| blan | ket | ad | dress | drag | on | cat | kin |
| com | ic | trip | lets | trum | pet | hab | it |
| a | cross | matt | ress | prob | lem | ton | sil |
| vel | vet | in | fant | chil | dren | mas | ter |

**Two-syllable words—digraphs, final e, vowel at end of syllable**

| | | | | | | | |
|---|---|---|---|---|---|---|---|
| be | long | mor | ning | pave | ment | car | pet |
| pic | ture | num | ber | mis | take | um | pire |
| sen | tence | gar | den | cray | on | Sun | day |
| lit | tle | am | use | trac | tor | cos | tume |

**Adding simple endings—no doubling**

| **ing**<br>**ed** | | **er** | | **er**<br>**est** | **y** | **ful** |
|---|---|---|---|---|---|---|
| need | train | dust | read | cold | rain | sin |
| nail | wheel | farm | steam | light | frost | fit |
| spoil | roar | heat | hunt | warm | soap | wish |
| seem | heat | learn | sing | deep | dirt | power |
| fear | cook | cook | train | bright | mist | |

| ish | en | some |
|---|---|---|
| boy | gold | tire |
| imp | fright | |
| girl | wood | **ty** |
| child | light | safe |

**Compound words**

| | | | | | | | |
|---|---|---|---|---|---|---|---|
| can | not | out | doors | some | body | play | time |
| up | set | | ward | | one | to | day |
| him | self | | side | | thing | | morrow |
| sun | set | | come | | where | rail | way |
| in | doors | mean | while | no | body | sun | shine |
| | ward | any | body | | one | | |
| | side | | one | | thing | | |
| | come | | thing | | where | | |
| | | | where | | | | |

# Part V—similar words often confused

**Remedial reading only**

Each word should be entered on a card and each group of similar word cards kept together. (Use of different coloured cards or type of card for each group is helpful.) The cards should be practised regularly, preferably in teacher-supervised groups. The teacher should point out clues to differentiation—phonic, linguistic or mnemonic.

usual usually unusual unusually

either neither

with what when which

could should would

his this

he the then when

quit quiet quite

here where there

at that what

they there their

of for from form off

though through thought thorough

# Appendix 1—use of SPELLING PATTERNS as a remedial reading programme

(as successfully used with dyslexic and other students for over twelve years)

**Alphabet sounds**
First teach basic letter sounds and blending of three to five letter single (short) vowel words. (There are many books and games to help but I have found the *Stott Programmed Reading Kit* (Holmes McDougall) most useful.)

**SPELLING PATTERNS pages 4—34**
**1 Using the Dr. Seuss Beginner Books (Collins)**
(chosen because their appeal is ageless and culture-free)
The student should work systematically through SPELLING PATTERNS up to page 34. The order of presentation of patterns is based on the words needed to read the *Dr. Seuss Beginner Books* listed below, and is programmed so that each step logically succeeds and reinforces previous steps.

The student should read each book after mastering the relevant word patterns and the extra sight words set out below—e.g. *Green Eggs and Ham* can be read after reaching page 20 in this book, provided that the sight words supplied up to page 20 are also taught.

**Sight words for Dr. Seuss books**
(page) **4** some was the to **5** are he ball into **7** boy said **8** you were they would could should **9** any many be **11** England we **12** one two three four five six seven eight nine ten eleven by fire **15** saw **16** want *Green Eggs and Ham* **21** walk talk stalk chalk **23** who *Hop on Pop* **25** ace face lace pace place race gone **26** when circus blue orange violet *Put Me in the Zoo*; *Ten Apples up on Top* **27** why do have **28** women shoe **29** some someone something somehow somewhere go we're *Snow*; *Are You My Mother?* **30** water honey bear friend come *The Big Honey Hunt*; *Robert the Rose Horse* **31** rough machine country before *Sam and the Firefly*; *One Fish, Two Fish*; *A Big Ball of String*; *The Big Jump* **33** once more **34** true Mr. *The King, the Mice and the Cheese*; *The Cat in the Hat*; *The Cat in the Hat Comes Back*

**2 Using any other reading scheme**
Go through the scheme, listing the words used. Sort these into spelling pattern groups and sight words. (Words which have a spelling used only once or twice in the scheme.) Teach the spelling patterns in the order required for the scheme used and ensure that the sight words are practised.

**3 After the Beginner Books or reading scheme**
Once the student has a sufficient foundation to read at a level of six and a half years reading age, let him read any book of his choice in which he needs to be told about six new words a lesson. Always tell him the new words while he is reading, but list them and practise them later. Note any spelling groups involved and teach them by using the relevant pages of SPELLING PATTERNS.

**Dyslexic and other students with exceptional difficulties**
Most remedial students will be able to *read* (but not necessarily recall for spelling) the words covered in the exercises. Where there are severe memory problems, however, two further procedures are helpful.

**1 check cards**
Make a card containing each spelling pattern as it is learned. Check recall sound(s) associated with the letter groups learned so far every lesson until automatic recognition is firmly established (about one term).
**2 reading dictionary**
The student enters every word he was told during reading into an alphabetically indexed notebook. (Using the usual procedure for writing words—see notes for teachers.) Reading of these words is checked every lesson until the student has read them correctly in three consecutive lessons. Marks are entered after the word in pencil and deleted when a word is forgotten. (Keep your sense of humour and make it a game. Words often forgotten should be learned in other ways. This very rarely arises.)

**Lesson plan**
Each lesson should contain
**1** check on recall of things learned so far
**2** new reading and/or topic writing
**3** teaching a new spelling pattern group
**4** success
**5** praise.
At some time during each week there should also be
**1** 'fun' reading (easy books)
**2** taped stories which the student can hear and read simultaneously
**3** serial reading of a good story by the teacher (to *all* ages of students).

## Appendix 2—notes for teachers

**1** SPELLING PATTERNS is relevant to all ages of student over seven years who need help with spelling patterns as predictable letter groups, from junior school to adult class. The practice exercises are deliberately kept simple as their sole purpose is to aid the student to practise seeing, hearing and writing the words and the predictable patterns therein. Illustrations are deliberately simple outline drawings to encourage the student to visualise for himself. Exercises asking the student to illustrate a word are for the same purpose, and are as valuable to older students as to younger ones.

**2** These spelling patterns were collected as the need for them arose, to explain the reading and spelling of the words involved and to simplify words often thought to lack any system. Approximately eighty per cent of English words are regular according to some pattern. SPELLING PATTERNS, together with LOGICAL SPELLING, endeavours to present English words in a systematic way which will aid recall. Word lists are not exhaustive. Extra words fitting each spelling pattern should be entered as they arise.

**3** The spelling pattern groups are presented in graded steps so that if Part I is worked through in sequence the student is not required to read or spell any words not previously covered in the book. Part II (consonant patterns) is not graded but is presented in alphabetical order for easy reference. These patterns generally cause less difficulty than patterns containing vowels and can be done as the need arises.

Students not needing the full programmed course can use the whole book for reference and practice in particular areas causing difficulty.

**4** Each student should have
a blank note book for the spelling book
another note book for the exercises
a pencil and rubber or a biro and ink rubber.

**5 Learning the words**

**a** The teacher first discusses the letter group and pronounces it clearly. The students then repeat it in their own speech. (This avoids any dialect problems as the students are learning the spelling which relates to their own pronunciation.)
**b** The teacher then reads the list of words.
**c** Teacher and students read the words together.
**d** The student then reads the words to himself and chooses a key word for the illustration in his spelling book.

**6 Writing the words**

Must always be from memory. The student may first study each word as long as he likes. He should
**a** look at and say the word
**b** when he thinks he knows it, write it (without looking at the original)
**c** check it
**d** if wrong, erase and repeat steps a–c.
**Never** allow alterations. An error should be erased. Joined handwriting should be used as soon as possible.

**7 Making the spelling book**

An ordinary notebook with blank pages is best. The student uses a double page for each spelling pattern, heading each page clearly with the letters. He then writes the words (from memory as in 6 above) on one side and draws a key picture (his own choice) on the opposite page.
Notes 5–7 form the procedure for Exercise 1 throughout the book.

**8** Tests (pages 114–17) can be dictated by the teacher, a tape recorder or another student.

An additional helpful exercise is for the students to compose their own story, poem or nonsense passage using as many of the words listed as possible.

**9** Words boxed within the lists for the spelling patterns are words containing the same spelling patterns but different pronunciations.

**10** *Joined handwriting* should be taught and used as soon as possible as it aids recall of a word and reduces reversal problems such as b and d. Always encourage the student to write a whole word.

**11** All exercises involving sentences should be answered by writing the full sentence.

Answers are given on pages 118–21. A different answer is permissible if it fits the clue and the relevant letter group.

Typing the spelling book is helpful to many students. An appeal to parents or local firms often brings a free typewriter.

**12** A clear, analytical approach to the letter groups and a precise use of language in explanations is essential. Particular attention should be paid by both the teacher and student to the use of terms such as
letter sound symbol digraph word phrase sentence paragraph.

## Index